French Theatre Today

Theatre Today Series also includes:

Disrupting the Spectacle: Five Years of Experimental and Fringe Theatre in Britain   Peter Ansorge
Playwrights' Theatre   The English Stage Company at the Royal Court Theatre   Terry Browne
American Playwrights 1945–75   Catharine Hughes
African Theatre Today   Martin Banham

Garry O'Connor

French Theatre Today

with a Foreword by Harold Hobson

Pitman Publishing

28364

First published 1975

Sir Isaac Pitman and Sons Ltd
Pitman House, 39 Parker Street, London WC2B 5PB, UK
Pitman Medical Publishing Co Ltd
42 Camden Road, Tunbridge Wells, Kent TN1 2QD, UK
Focal Press Ltd
31 Fitzroy Square, London W1P 6BH, UK
Pitman Publishing Corporation
6 East 43 Street, New York, NY 10017, USA
Fearon Publishers Inc
6 Davis Drive, Belmont, California 94002, USA
Pitman Publishing Pty Ltd
Pitman House, 158 Bouverie Street, Carlton, Victoria 3053, Australia
Pitman Publishing
Copp Clark Publishing
517 Wellington Street West, Toronto M5V 1G1, Canada
Sir Isaac Pitman and Sons Ltd
Banda Street, PO Box 46038, Nairobi, Kenya
Pitman Publishing Co SA (Pty) Ltd
Craighall Mews, Jan Smuts Avenue, Craighall Park,
Johannesburg 2001, South Africa

Cased edition ISBN 0 273 00349 6
Paperback edition ISBN 0 273 00292 9

Text set in 11 pt. Photon Imprint, printed by photolithography,
and bound in Great Britain at The Pitman Press, Bath

(G. 3540/3517:13)

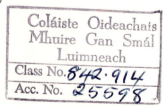

foreword

This is a book of great penetration, and also of courage and of independent judgement. That Garry O'Connor recognizes, as very few
British critics do, that Jean Genet is one of the greatest writers in
France today is an assurance of his delicate responses to the glories,
subtle beneath their surface crudeness, of the French language. It
also confirms confidence in the firmness of his independent judgement. But this is not all. For with Genet he couples Jean Anouilh, a
dramatist immensely fashionable for a short while after the true
significance of his *Antigone* had been misunderstood, but who then
passed into a period in which he suffered the contempt and hostility of
men too crass in mind to appreciate the terrible violence of his
lacerated spirit. Mr O'Connor restores Anouilh to proper honour.

What will immediately strike any reader of Mr O'Connor's book is
the depth of understanding, not only of French literature, but also of
French society, from which he writes. Especially in his brilliant
chapter on Jean-Paul Sartre, but also in many other sections of his
study, he constantly reminds us that the French theatre is an aspect
of society. In its great days just after the war the French theatre was
a politically committed theatre, and a consideration of this leads Mr
O'Connor to several perceptive social observations, some of which
will considerably surprise British readers. His remarks on the effect
of nationalization on French industry are particularly worth
considering.

One of the chief merits of this remarkable book is, in fact, its
realization of the connection between theatre and politics, a realization all the more striking because, though Mr O'Connor writes with
passion and concern (and often with beauty, as in his final sad comments on Samuel Beckett), he is also without discernible prejudice.
Even when he writes about so ambiguous a man as Montherlant, for
whom he has a not indefensible admiration, he can be read without
increase of blood pressure, and with a deepening of understanding,
both by those who accept, and those who regard as loathsome,
Montherlant's political and social convictions.

Mr O'Connor's book is particularly illuminating to those students
of French theatre whose interest is chiefly in avant-garde work.
French Theatre Today by no means ignores the boulevard. In fact
the opening chapter is a fascinating account of just how the popular
part of the French theatre organizes itself. But what is alive today in
the French theatre is not the popular popular theatre, that is, the
theatre to which people go, but the unpopular popular theatre, that
is, the theatre to which all intellectuals think that people should go,
but from which people usually stay away. Trekking out to Nanterre,
or beyond the immense and famous waste of Père Lachaise in search

of some ill-performed and uncomfortably housed social and political drama by an unknown author who nevertheless some day may be a world luminary, is a daunting activity, and in English at any rate Mr O'Connor is the only critic I know who provides a comprehensive view of what we should find at the end of our pilgrimage, if only we had the strength and determination to make it.

Until recently, avant-garde theatre has not been easy to learn about, even in France itself. The critics of the great newspapers have devoted far less of their attention to avant-garde work in Paris than the critics of London dailies and weeklies have given to English avant-garde drama. Moreover French avant-garde productions have suffered from the fact that Jean-Jacques Gautier, of the Académie Française, who is far and away the most influential of French critics, has a very poor opinion of them. M. Gautier is the most genial of men, but he writes in short, sharp sentences that hit on the head with hammer blows anything that displeases him. French avant-garde theatre therefore follows a thorny critical path. But, fortunately for us, Mr O'Connor knows every inch of it, so that his chapters upon relatively, or in this country wholly, unknown dramatists, are a peculiarly invaluable part of his invaluable work.

HAROLD HOBSON

Acknowledgements

I am grateful to the following for their kind permission to quote from copyright material: Mr Peter Brook and Penguin Books for quotations from an introduction to *Ring Round The Moon* and *The Empty Space*; M. Jean Anouilh and his translator Lucienne Hill for quotations from *Becket* and *The Goldfish*; Mr Samuel Beckett for quotations from *Malone Dies, Molloy, Waiting For Godot, Endgame, Proust*, and translations of Mexican poetry; Gerald Duckworth & Co. Ltd for a quotation from *Awakenings* by Oliver Sachs; Thames and Hudson for quotations from Barrault's *Memories for Tomorrow*, translated by Jonathan Griffin; Methuen & Co. Ltd for a quotation from Sartre's *Crime Passionel*, translated by Kitty Black; Faber & Faber Ltd for quotations from Genet's *Reflections on the Theatre*, translated by Richard Seaver, and Genet's *The Maids* (translator Bernard Frechtman), as well as from T. S. Eliot's *Collected Poems 1909–1962*; Penguin Books Ltd for quotations from Martin Esslin's *The Theatre of the Absurd* and Sartre's *The Trojan Women* (translated by Ronald Duncan); the editors of *Theatre Quarterly* for quotations from an article by M. Arthur Adamov (translated by David Bradby) and an interview with M. Roger Planchon (interviewed by Michael Kustow).

Except for the quotations acknowledged on this page the translations are my own. I should like to thank Mr Jeremy Treglown for reading the manuscript and Mrs Janet Kite for typing it. And I am deeply grateful to the *Financial Times* and its successive Arts Editors, John Higgins, Anthony Curtis, and B. A. Young, for their encouragement.

The Chart of Important Productions 1940–75 is based in part on a similar table from Larousse's *Dictionary of French Contemporary Theatre*.

To Victoria

Contents

	Foreword by Harold Hobson	v
	Acknowledgements	vii
1	**Finance and organization**	1
2	**Influences**	11
3	**Theatre of choice (1)** Sartre	22
4	**Theatre of choice (2)** Montherlant, Michel, Césaire, Yacine	35
5	**The cynics (1)** Adamov, Ionesco	40
6	**The cynics (2)** Weingarten, Vian, Tardieu, Arrabal	45
7	**Dislocated consciousness** Samuel Beckett	51
8	**Language and silence** Genet, Marguerite Duras	56
9	**Jeunes auteurs (1)** Adrien, Atlan, Haïm, Grumberg	62
10	**Jeunes auteurs (2)** Ehni, Cousin, Benedetto, Vinaver, Café-théâtre	69
11	**Jean Anouilh**	75
12	**Directors** Bourseiller, Barrault, Blin, Serreau, Vilar, Planchon, Chéreau, Savary, Mnouchkine	82
	Postscript on French acting	92
	Chart of important productions 1940–75	96
	Further reading	110
	Selected list of plays	113
	Index	116

'. . . the pull of French life on the imagination and on the habit of mind is so immensely strong because it is founded on the secret places of the intellect. The intellectual or reflective life is not necessarily a dull thing; to a bold thinker the problems of human life can be as thrilling as any physical pursuit. But the Anglo-Saxon male never gets beyond intellectual adolescence because whether at home or at school the whole pressure of the educational machinery from which he suffers is directed towards eliminating intellectual adventure.'

FORD MADOX FORD, 1926

'People now extol only what is new, only what produces a shock, causes "an event". They no longer know for whom or for what they are working. The profession is bewildered, like a team of horses being pulled this way and that. Luckily desire is always reborn, the need still makes itself felt, and we go on working desperately.'

J.-L. BARRAULT, 1974

1 Finance and organization

'For if you set out to mention everything you would never be done,
and that's what counts, to be done, to have done. Oh I know, even
when you mention only a few of the things there are, you do not
get done either, I know, I know.'

Samuel Beckett

The field is of a daunting size. There are 380 authors mentioned in
the contemporary dictionary of French Men of the Theatre published
by the French Theatre Centre. A preliminary list of established
playwrights to be covered might include Achard, Anouilh, Barillet
and Grédy, Audiberti, Deval, Marceau, Montherlant, Pagnol,
Passeur, Roger-Ferdinand, Roussin, Salacrou, Sarment, Sartre,
Sauvajon, Thomas, Zimmer ... One might make another, more
avant-garde list, starting with Adamov: Adamov, Arrabal, Beckett,
Billetdoux, Cousin, Dubillard, Duras, Foissy, Gatti, Genet, Ionesco,
Obaldia, Schéhadé, Tardieu, Vauthier, Vinaver, Weingarten,
Yacine. . . .

Even so, one would not have touched upon two other significant
sources of dramatic output: novelists who have turned to the theatre;
and philosophers. Among the former are Aymé, Druon, Green,
Mauriac, Maurois, Romains, Sagan, Vailland; among the latter, De
Beauvoir, Camus, Garaudy, Marcel, Maulnier. And then one would
have neglected the poets: Cocteau, Michaux, Pichette . . .

In one American university alone, there is a collection of over
7,000 French plays on microfilm, and this collection grows at the rate
of over 600 a year. Yet it is fashionable to belittle or ignore, at least in
this country, even in France itself, recent work by French authors. In
the Amiens Manifesto of 1969, there is a plaintive cry from eleven
'jeunes auteurs' who are unhappy at the general attitude towards
new writing. These eleven, Guy Foissy, Jean-Claude Grumberg, Victor Haïm, Georges Michel, Janine Worms, Pierre Halet, Marguerite
Duras, Jean-Pierre Faye, René Ehni, Romain Weingarten, Gabriel
Cousin, point out that for every performance of a new French work in
France, there are ten abroad, most of them in Germany and other
European countries.

Jean Cocteau has pointed out that 'in the theatre, success always
comes from a misunderstanding', and it may well be that the very
lack of recognition of new playwrights is helping them to forge a distinctive personality, to measure up in time to the avant-garde of the
fifties, who have now become eminent and honoured old men, and
even academicians, like Eugène Ionesco. Most of the new writers
have at best a minority appeal. Since the beginning of time there have
been few good plays and few good playwrights, and one may be

1

making a mistake in thinking that, because there is more money at
the disposal of the arts today, the volume of excellence must
necessarily increase.

In France, as in England, there are two attitudes to running
theatres and putting on plays. The first is that theatre is a commodity
which must be invested in, bought and sold, promoted and used to
make a profit, if it is to survive. The lame ducks are killed off ruthlessly, the successes boosted and encouraged to run for ever. The second
attitude is that the theatre is a branch of education, and, as such,
must be subsidized, for only by this means can valuable work be
presented which would otherwise be condemned to decay. The
didactic aspect of this attitude, which once used to represent that of
the sponsors or patrons, whether they were the State, the
aristocracy, the Crown, or the Jesuit fathers, has since the Second
World War been usurped by the left wing. When Kenneth Tynan
asked Jean-Paul Sartre in 1961 whether right-wing writers could not
create works of art, Sartre replied 'No. Because today, although the
"Right" controls events still, in the sense that it has power, it has lost
the capacity to understand them. It has abandoned most of its old
ideals and hasn't replaced them; it doesn't understand the nature of
its adversaries.' This may seem bigoted and blind, but is nevertheless
a widely held view.

As in England, new subsidized work is very often anti-
authoritarian and anti-State, or, in other words, directed against its
patron, and directed against the beliefs of most of its tax-paying
citizens. In France, the positive Marxist alternatives seem to be more
widely aired and better understood. Another of the ironies of the subsidized method is that it is usually the popular successes of
yesteryear which become the classics of today, and which are
therefore presented in the State-subsidized theatres. So the new
classics do still tend to come from the private sector. Sartre's own plays
have enjoyed, and still do enjoy, popular commercial success as much
as the comedies of Roussin or Félicien Marceau.

The following figures are from a budget for fifty performances of a
play in 1971, in a commercial boulevard theatre. In France a play's
budget is based upon the performance itself rather than the week of
performances, and returns are made separately. The prices in this
theatre, which has 450 seats, range from 8 to 33 francs (they have
risen sharply, and the range is in 1973–4 more usually from 12 to 50).
The figures come from Geneviève Rozental's excellent *Notes et
Etudes Documentaires* Nos. 3907–8. The exchange rate for the
sterling equivalents is, in 1973, 11 francs to the pound (4½ francs to
the dollar).

Running costs	1,600F (£145) × 50
Actors' salaries (4) and social security	1,200F (£110) × 50
Director's salary	87F (£8) × 50
Designer's fee	3,000F (£272)
Production and publicity costs	76,650F (£6,970)
Total	220,000F (£20,000)

In addition to these costs, or, rather, before these costs can be recouped from the daily takings at the box office, there are the authors' rights to be paid (13 per cent), and value-added tax (7·5 per cent). Therefore there must be 6,000F (£545) every night in the box office for the play to break even. This means, in terms of an audience, that the theatre must be either filled with students, or cut-price block-bookings, or half filled with people who pay the full price. The same theatre's general manager has stated that in an average year the loss is in the region of 150,000F (£13,000), assuming they have not met with outstandingly bad luck.

Independent producers, like subsidized theatres, sell their shows to other theatres (the equivalent in England is called a 'guarantee'). The price can range from under £200 a night for a modest production, to over £3,500 for a big and prestigious musical. In the Maisons de la Culture (regional arts centres), all productions are booked on this basis, and the average price is 8,000F (over £700). A company is an expensive and often unaffordable luxury because union rules have stipulated that an actor must be paid a minimum of 1,520F (£140) a month, to which has to be added 45 per cent social insurance and security tax. A company of a dozen actors, even at the lowest possible reckoning, would cost in the region of £30,000 a year. As Jean Vilar has said, 'You must pay actors. Don't smile. . . . I know there are taxes and dues. But you must pay actors and pay them well. As much as possible. And make life pleasant for them. If not they won't be there to act (or rehearse) and they'll clear out as soon as they can.' Only companies such as Ariane Mnouchkine's Théâtre du Soleil can escape these stifling financial burdens by organizing themselves as a co-operative and paying their members a small fixed wage.

The principle of Maisons de la Culture was first set out in a circular issued by the drama director of the Ministry of Culture, Biasini, in the early sixties. 1963 saw the opening of the first batch of theatres, at Le Havre, Caen, and Bourges, in old buildings adapted to house the arts. Then followed others, purpose-built: Amiens, Thonon, Grenoble, which was designed by Wogensky, Firminy, designed by Le Corbusier, Saint-Etienne, Rennes. The principal idea behind this innovation was to bring culture to towns which previously had no organized activities, and the priority in each Maison was a theatre which could be used for concerts and films, as well as plays. The first problem with this costly new conception was to attract people to work in them, and this was done through Government subsidy to a theatrical company; as a result other activities came to take second place to the theatre. Another problem resulted from the conflict in sources of income. The Government subsidies, as in England, had no strings attached, but the municipal authorities, who also gave grants, objected to the political or aesthetic slant of the work presented. Some of these authorities, notably those at Caen and Bourges, took advantage of the reaction against the student uprising in May 1968, and sacked their directors. Those directors who now feel that Maisons de la Culture should play an essential part in the transformation of society are having a thin time.

In the table set out on p. 4 is shown, from French Ministerial sources, the sums spent by the Government on theatres outside Paris (in a scheme called the 'décentralisation dramatique'), in 1971.

	Sum spent	
Name of Theatre	F	£
Théâtre de L'Est Parisien	3,000,000	263,000
Théâtre National de Strasbourg	2,700,000	245,000
Théâtre de la Cité (Villeurbanne)	1,900,000	172,000
Comédie de Saint-Etienne	1,800,000	163,000
Action Culturelle du Sud-Est (Marseille)	1,550,000	131,000
Théâtre de Nice	1,400,000	127,000
Grenier de Toulouse	1,300,000	118,000
Comédie de Caen	1,300,000	118,000
Théâtre de Cothurne (Lyon)	1,300,000	118,000
Comédie de L'ouest (Rennes)	1,050,000	95,000
Tréteaux de France	1,000,000	90,000
Théâtre de Lambrequin (Tourcoing)	800,000	72,000
Théâtre du Midi (Carcassonne)	800,000	72,000
Théâtre de Bourgogne (Beaune)	750,000	68,000
Comédie des Alpes (Grenoble)	500,000	45,000
Centre Théâtral de Franche-Comte (Besançon)	400,000	36,000
Centre Théâtral du Limousin (Limoges)	400,000	36,000
Théâtre des Pays de Loire (Angers)	400,000	36,000
Théâtre des Amandiers (Nanterre)	400,000	36,000
Théâtre de la Commune (Aubervilliers)	400,000	36,000
Théâtre Populaire des Flandres (Lille)	300,000	27,000
Total	23,450,000	2,130,000

These figures, it must be remembered, may be large by English standards, but are small compared to the sums spent on theatres in central Paris. The City of Paris, for example, spent in 1971 alone 4,750,000F on the Théâtre de la Ville (over £430,000). France has a much older tradition of State support for the theatre than England: the first company to receive a grant was the Troupe Royale in 1639; later, Molière's company took over that title while other companies playing in Paris received regular subsidy; in 1680 Louis XIV founded the Comédie-Française, and since then there has been an unbroken succession of National Theatres. The original Odéon was built by Peyre and Wailly round about 1780 for what were then called the Comédiens Français. During the Revolution, the revolutionaries split with the royalists and moved over to the Palais Royal, which was named Théâtre du Peuple, and then Théâtre Egalité. Evenings in the theatre were subsidized and made available free of charge. But recently the sums of subsidy have increased enormously. In 1971 the budget of the Ministry of Culture was in the order of £60½ million (665 millions F) and, in 1972, grants for the theatre increased by 22·5 per cent. Out of the 1971 figure, over 80 millions F (£7·2 million) was spent on the theatre. The forecasts for the three major State-subsidized theatres in Paris, in 1972, are shown on p. 5.

If this table is compared with the previous one it can be seen that there is rather more spent every year on the three theatres in Paris than on the twenty-one main provincial centres. Most of these enor-

Name of Theatre	Sum F	£
Comédie-Française	16,244,850	1,476,000
Théâtre Nationale Populaire	5,760,170	523,000
Odéon	5,125,000	466,000
Superannuation fund for the Comédie-Française	1,006,000	91,000
Works (rebuilding, etc.)	4,000,000	363,000
Total	32,136,020	2,921,000

mous sums go on the administrative costs of running them: of the 325 people employed by the Comédie-Française, only 70 are actors; neither the TNP, which used to be at the Palais de Chaillot, nor the Théâtre de France at the Odéon has a permanent company, and yet the former, without actors, has a staff of 128, the latter 94. It is hardly surprising that the National Theatres in Paris have a distinctly bureaucratic flavour.

Paris is not a city with a distinctive silhouette; but when one forms a mental picture of it, more often than not it comes out as a ground plan with the Seine snaking through the centre, separating the right bank from the left with the finality of an international frontier. There are between 52 and 55 privately owned theatres, and, as can be seen from the plan, most of these are clustered north of the Opéra, and in Montmartre. These are the strongholds of bourgeois theatre.

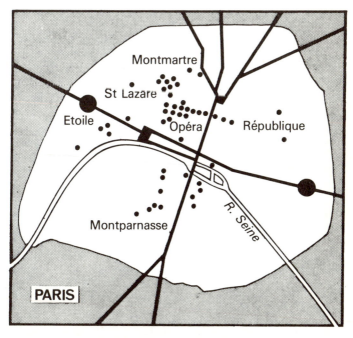

Position of the Theatres of Paris
(Each dot represents a permanent theatre)

Going to them is very different from going to West End commercial theatres in London, for not only are prices much more expensive, but you are expected to tip the lady who shows you to your seat, and she is rarely satisfied with less than two or three francs (20 or 30p). Programmes cost, on an average, 5F (approx 50p), but there is the advantage that, at certain theatres, this includes the text of the play. Very few performances start before 9 p.m. and the average evening lasts until midnight or longer. There is not the almost obligatory demand, as in London, that no play should run more than $2\frac{1}{2}$ hours.

It is often said there are too many theatres in Paris: indeed it has been pointed out that, if every play put on received glowing notices, there would not be enough of a playgoing public to fill them. There may be still more theatres than in London or New York, but there has been a huge fall-off in attendance: 3 million seats were sold in commercial theatres in 1970, while twelve years before, in 1958, $4\frac{1}{4}$ million were sold.

Only one fifth of the French ever go to the theatre, while of these not more than 20 per cent go more than six times a year. The cinema, by contrast, is frequented by 63 per cent of the population. Theatregoers are dominantly young people, except at the boulevard theatre, where the audience consists often of up to 60 per cent of people over fifty years of age, while in the 'théâtres populaires' between 58 and 68 per cent of the audience consists of people under thirty.

French audiences as a whole fall into four categories, according to *The Theatre and its Public*, a survey conducted by the Ministry of Culture in 1964, and summarized by Mlle Rozental. These are:

(1) the middle-class public who love fashionable shows, amusing comedies, in prestigious surroundings, such as the Paris right bank theatres clustered together in the diagram;

(2) the middle and lower middle-class audiences who are more modest in their social aspirations, and whose taste is generally broader, though they still place the accent heavily on entertainment;

(3) the university public (teachers and students) who go to plays connected with their fields of interest, or the traditionally 'intellectual' theatre; and finally

(4) the so-called 'popular' audience, which consists of the more intelligent working-class namely union officials and stenographers according to this research, clerical workers, minor civil servants, and the intellectual professions.

What this public is offered differs enormously from place to place, and season to season. The variety and scope shown, for example, in one week of the Comédie-Française are astonishing. It was possible, in a week sampled at random, to see three plays by Molière, one by Marivaux, one by Montherlant, as well as Corneille's *Le Cid*, and four curtain raisers. The organizational power of assembling so many different teams is remarkable, although in quality the theatre leans too heavily on some of the great *sociétaires* such as Robert Hirsch and has often been criticized for depending upon its stars. Nevertheless, to strike and set ten diverse plays, as well as costume them, is a Herculean accomplishment. The Comédie's holy temple aspect, its special box held in perpetual readiness—and invariable emptiness—for the President of the Republic, with or without his

Prime Minister, continues, and its *fonctionnaires* still scrutinize the audiences to make sure they are properly dressed, much as their priestly counterparts once used to do in Nôtre Dame. The latter now seem to have abandoned this practice.

At the opposite end of the scale from the Comédie-Française is one of France's most active and progressive theatres, the Théâtre de l'Est Parisien (known as the TEP) situated at Gambetta, an eastern suburb of Paris. The TEP was built up to its present eminence by Guy Rétoré, who, some years ago, as a thirty-year-old amateur actor with a job in French Railways, after failing twice to enter the Conservatoire—the school attached to the Comédie-Française—formed his own group. This was called the Guild, and at first its members acted anonymously.

Born and bred in the 20th arrondissement, Rétoré is a firm believer in popular theatre, and in what he calls the cultural 'decentralization' of Paris. He pioneered this movement, starting modestly, and finally winning recognition when the Ministry of Culture gave him this large and superbly equipped theatre to direct, as Paris' first centre for the arts. Beginning with 1,000 members in 1963, the centre now has 27,000 members and a yearly audience of over a quarter of a million. Its repertoire leans heavily on little-known classics such as Victor Hugo's *Marie Tudor*, or adaptations, like Jean Cosmos' adaptation of Gogol's *The Overcoat*; in production style it has more in common with Jean Vilar than with Roger Planchon.

Sartre has written, in *Théâtre épique et théâtre dramatique*, that the newspaper critic holds his position by virtue of the degree to which he reflects his readers' views in his own. In France the critics of the daily papers wield the greatest power, namely Jean-Jacques Gautier of *Le Figaro*, the former critic, B. Poireot-Delpech, of *Le Monde* and, after them, the critics of *France-Soir, L'Aurore, Combat*. The weeklies have a certain degree of influence, notably *L' Express, Paris-Match, Le Nouvel Observateur*, but there is considerably less critical coverage of the theatre than in England. There is occasionally more coverage in depth, for example when *Le Monde* devotes a whole weekend supplement to it.

French critics are, as far as one can generalize, more ruthless than their English counterparts, far more abrupt, dismissive, and patronizing, and less prone to overpraise. Far less space is allocated in the press to new work, and to experiment. This may be why the new theatre in France has gained so little identity, for there is little by way of an articulate minority speaking up for it. The reverse is the case in England, where the critic's identity is inflated, and some praise indiscriminately. Kenneth Tynan wrote in *Twilight of a Critic* 'Why bother to make history if you can earn a better living as a non-combatant observer?'

My intention in the following chapters is to explore three main influences at work in the French theatre today. These are the literary, the surrealist, and the socialist, or, broadly speaking, the influences of Claudel, Artaud, and Brecht. There are, in my opinion, four outstanding playwrights still alive, but three of these, Beckett, Genet, and Sartre, have ceased to produce major work, while the fourth, Anouilh, is as prolific as ever. There is, in addition, Montherlant, who is a major writer; he died only recently, and the production of *La Ville dont le prince est un enfant*, in 1968, is as important in recent French theatre as that of Claudel's *Tête d'or* in 1959. There are only two American playwrights comparable to these five, and these are Williams and Miller. In England, the conditions and style of production are far superior to those in France, yet there are no living English playwrights of their stature. Fry and Rattigan are both alive, yet their present influence is negligible. Coward is probably the latest great English playwright. There are a number—Arden, Pinter, Wesker, Osborne, Stoppard, Storey—whose influences and statures can be compared to those of Camus, Ionesco, Adamov, Césaire, Vian, Gatti, Duras, Weingarten, who are all at the moment important figures in French theatre. The American playwrights, Edward Albee, Leroi Jones, Jack Richardson, and Jack Gelber, make a disappointing comparison.

The form of theatre flourishing in England and America at this moment is the 'fringe' or 'underground'. The vitality here is exciting, even if it lacks form and direction, and, more crucially, compassion or understanding. High on the list of fringe activities in France are companies like Mnouchkine's Théâtre du Soleil and Savary's Grand Magic Circus (Chapter 12). Then there is the café-théâtre, although this is unsubsidized and very much a half-hearted affair compared with lunchtime theatres in London or off-off Broadway of the La Mama variety. Fringe theatre is on the whole—a good example is the plays of Sam Shepard—an expression of permissiveness and the spirit of disorder at their most extreme. French society is not as permissive, and is unlikely ever to be, as English and American society. Permissiveness is not a Gallic or Latin tendency, and its root is essentially in the more puritan disposition of Anglo-Saxon races. Paradoxically it is Barrault, now in his sixties, who is still one of the most revolutionary figures in the French theatre.

Nevertheless there is considerable pressure on France from the larger and more dominant English-speaking world, both in the commercial sectors and in the cultural world, especially theatre and film. Therefore there are an immense number of imported works at any one time. In the theatre some years ago most new plays seemed to be English or American, but now the situation has changed. The Anglo-American imports are sex shows, which once used to be a symbol of French sophistication.

Comparisons *are* difficult. One could argue that no play written in England since 1950 is as great as *Waiting for Godot*, yet one has to remember that while *Look Back in Anger* was a success in London and New York, in Paris *Waiting for Godot* to begin with played to empty houses. It has taken time for Beckett's influence to permeate, and the influence is probably greater as a result. Stoppard's *Rosencrantz and Guildenstern are Dead*, resoundingly successful on both sides of the Atlantic, was a complete flop in Paris. Wesker's *The Kitchen*, which has never been a commercial success in London, was the outstanding play of 1967 in Paris; its naturalism was stealthily transmuted, in Ariane Mnouchkine's production, into a very poetic and pure piece of behaviourism of which Jacques Copeau would have been proud. Ionesco's *Les Chaises*, and *La Leçon* have had as world-wide an influence as anything Pinter ever wrote, while the whole working-class naturalism which George Devine pioneered at the Royal Court, and whose latest expression is in David Storey's cool and painstaking canvasses of family or working life, was killed off in France some fifty or so years ago. André Antoine, the great pre-First World War exponent of naturalism, is reputed to have generously said to Jacques Copeau, the innovator of the defined and 'poetic' production style which superseded the Théâtre-Libre, 'ride us down'. Copeau was the precursor, in France, of the directors of 'Le Cartel', and, in England, of Michel Saint-Denis, Peter Brook, and Peter Hall.

Where the new generation of writers in England is concerned, Artaud is far more influential than any previous English writer, and Genet's view of the saintliness of criminality, destroying as it does the 'obscene' structures of organized society, has been widely adopted, without resulting in any new or significant form or development, and without really accurately mirroring English society. To this extent, in spirit certainly and often even in style and content, the work of many of these writers is far less 'experimental' or 'original' than the theorist practitioners of new form in the twenties and thirities, and the philosopher-playwrights such as Sartre, De Beauvoir, Camus, of the forties and fifties. Indeed, if there is a crucial weakness of the new English and American drama, it is that there is little connection or relationship with an indigenous tradition. Its influences have been absorbed at a very eclectic and superficial level, and are often contrary to what the playwright is trying to say. The effect is often that of a crude irritant. It takes an artist as great as Brecht to practise eclecticism while retaining a unique individuality and a vision. A recent and interesting play like David Hare's *Knuckle* is marred by this lack of contact with immediate antecedents. English theatre is moving away from naturalism, which has hitherto been one of its strengths.

To point to another difference between English and French theatre one should perhaps briefly consider Pinter and Wesker. Both have a Jewish background, and a good deal of the rich and unique qualities in their work may come from their having found an earthy and accurate English context for an essentially Jewish and European sensibility. In Pinter's case this emerges in a Kafka-like sense of menace, in Wesker's, in the indomitable warmth of the family circle. But when Ionesco, Weingarten, Arrabal, Beckett, Adamov, adopted France as their culture, and French as their first language, either deliberately or through necessity, what they found was almost the reverse of what Pinter and Wesker found in England. They found not so much a context as a challenge, an intellectual climate which moulded them far more definitely into an existing tradition, and tested them far more rigorously. Thus they had the advantage not only of being new and avant-garde, but also of becoming immediately part of a tradition in which experiment was conducted along certain clearly determined lines.

The best experiment has really nothing to do with novelty. The more one looks at the most revolutionary plays of a generation such as *La Cantatrice chauve* or *Waiting for Godot*, the more one can see that the qualities which have made, and will make, them last are related strongly to their affinities with, and capacity for having absorbed, a strong tradition which has been alive in their immediate past.

Of the three influences, those of Artaud, Brecht, and Claudel which can be identified in the French theatre today, only the first two appear to be active in England and America. It may well be that the third, the influence of Claudel, is much nearer to the religious spirit in which drama originated. It is this influence which tends towards personalizing human conflict, making it awaken terror and compassion by sympathy with character, as opposed to the influences of Artaud and Brecht. The distinction must be made between Brecht's theoretical influence and his achievement; the influence is largely through the later and inferior plays, the powerful, theoretical writings and productions; his achievements as a playwright consist of the work produced in his early and middle periods.

Artaud's influence tends to accentuate the sensual elements of theatrical experience, and while Brecht's influence emphasizes the theoretically political impact and motive, both lead to a simplification of human conflict and result in the characters represented becoming, in the final reckoning, less human.

Predicting the course French theatre will follow in the future is as impossible as predicting the future course of society itself. Yet prediction consists largely of prognosis on the basis of existing trends and conditions. One of these is towards collective authorship of plays by groups such as the Living Theatre and the Théâtre du Soleil. Work so originated will probably only live as long as the group responsible for its creation is prepared to go on reviving it. Another trend is for plays that explore a change in social fashion, often for the shock value this can awaken. Into this category fall a large number of works about urban violence, women's liberation, homosexuality, fertility, contraception and so on. What will take their place are more plays about the new problems which will occupy the headlines of the future, and these new plays will also have a life only slightly less ephemeral than the headlines they supplement.

A crisis in Marxist belief might produce some fascinating plays, just as the great conflicts in religious and existential belief are at the heart of the greatest Western Drama. Solzhenitsyn's *One Day in the Life of Ivan Denisovich* and *The First Circle*, although novels, contain the seeds of Marxist drama. But before this could happen, more people would have to turn to Marxism, and Marxism would need to become both a more sophisticated and a more human belief than it is at present. In other words, it would need to come closer to reality as we know it.

The theatre is concerned with searching for something, and with finding something, whether this be, on the crudest level, a gun, or, more sophisticatedly, a secret, a principle, or a person. When the human race stops seeking, then the theatre will die. But it may die much earlier, if the search for purely material objectives persists, by being reduced to providing sensual solace and behaviouristic excitements.

2 Influences

'Between Claudel's theatre, which glorifies a human being as the sum total of organized "thinking dust", as he calls it, and the attitude of Artaud who subordinates word to the real action, there is a sharp contradiction.'

J.-P. Sartre

The Literary Influence

In the French theatre the word is still king and still reigns. Soon it may be reduced to the role of penitent courtier or abusive lackey. But for the moment it exerts its sway and its majesty, as can be seen from the considerable success, in Spring 1974, of two late, or little-known, works by formidable literary figures, Jacques Audiberti and Paul Claudel.

JACQUES AUDIBERTI (1899–1965) began writing for the stage in 1946, with *Quoat-quoat*; in 1947 *Le Mal court* (Evil is Spreading) won the prize of the 'jeunes compagnies', and the outstanding comédienne, Suzanne Flon, made her début in it. Most of Audiberti's twenty plays were first performed by 'jeunes compagnies', the equivalent of student or youth companies, and the best are *La Fête noire* (Black Festival, 1949), *Pucelle* (The Maid of Orleans, 1950), *La Hoberaute* (The Small Falcon, 1958) and *Le Cavalier seul* (The Lone Knight, 1963).

Audiberti's charm, first of all, is one of language. Correspondingly, his danger is that he can be over-florid. The revival of *Le Cavalier seul*, ten years after its production in Lyons, shows both the strength and weakness of his craft; he is carried away by his often blurred imagery, yet there is always something grandiose in the scheme, original in the means of expression.

The subject of *Le Cavalier seul* is religion, which Audiberti treats more as a social myth than a specific discipline; this has earned him the hostility of conservative critics. His depiction of Christ in *Le Cavalier seul* has something of the expression of Rouault's painting: absurdity in it, as well as suffering. The time is the eleventh century. There are three acts, and three locations—Languedoc, Byzantium, and Jerusalem. The hero Mirtus, a young peasant to begin with, becomes the Cavalier of the title by being pressed into service by a local landlord, the Count of Toulouse, and sent off on a crusade. He arrives at Byzantium and there Théopompe III and the Empress Zoë are so impressed by him that they offer him the crumbling empire. Although Mirtus is the only character who goes through all three acts, similar types crop up in each successive situation; his mother, for instance, becomes the Empress, his father the Autocrat, so that throughout his journey he is placed in the same kind of recurring

11

dilemma. But he refuses the responsibilities of power and moves on to Jerusalem, where Act II is set. In Act II there is a parody of the Passion, with two soldiers and a felon; Mirtus is offered, this time by the Divine Caliph, the command of the Saracen armies and the bed of the beautiful Fatima. Once more he is placed against the temptations of the flesh, the temptation of power, and again he refuses.

His final refusal is of the imaginary grace of God, offered in return for putting himself forward as a substitute for the man about to be crucified. He sends the latter to his death, rejecting Christianity and pleading for humanism. 'There's no one in the house of God,' he says, 'now there is someone.' He rejoins his own side in the Crusade and fights to capture the Holy Sepulchre.

Written in a very traditional style, *Le Cavalier seul*'s language is fertile, even flowery, reminiscent of Christopher Fry. When the hero, Mirtus, comes to Byzantium, he turns to the ruler, the autocrat Théopompe III, and says:

MIRTUS: Nous avons notre église, sans mosaïque, sans perles fines, toute pauvre et toute chaste comme la robe du maître éternel.

L'AUTOCRATE: (*see tâtant le bras*) Elle éclate. Cette fois, c'est clair, mon artère éclate. (*A Mirtus*) Mais vous vous en moquez, de votre église. Il suffit de vous regarder. J'ai touché ta joue. Elle sent la rose et la cendre.

MIRTUS: (*montrant Nérébis*) C'est l'odeur de cette roulure.

L'AUTOCRATE: Tais-toi! C'est une odeur qui provient de toi! C'est l'odeur de l'Orient! (*Il se coiffe de sa mitre*) Qu'il soit chrétien, hébreu, mongol ou musulman, l'Orient respecte le silence, le pouvoir et le désert du maître éternel. Vos prêtres latins, par contre, rabâchent que le maître éternal barbote dans votre soupe et que, sans cesse, il épie hommes et femmes dans le lit. Vos prêtres bénissent même, paraît-il, au nom du maître éternel, les dogues lâchés sur les chevreuils.

MIRTUS: We've our church, a church without mosaics, without fine pearls, poor and chaste like the robe of our eternal Lord.

THE AUTOCRAT: (*prodding his arm*) Bursting . . . obvious, this time, my artery's bursting. (*to Mirtus*) Oh you and your church! One only has to look at you. I've felt your cheek. It smells of roses and incense.

MIRTUS: (*showing Nerebis*) It's this trollop's smell . . .

THE AUTOCRAT: Shut up. It's your smell. It's the smell of the east. (*He coifs his hair with his mitre.*) Whether Christian, Hebrew, Mongol, or Muslim, the east respects the silence, the power, and the isolation of the Lord. But look at your latin priests: they keep harping on that the Lord splashes about in soup and spies on men and women in bed. Your priests even bless, it seems, in the name of the Lord, the very dogs they unleash after deer.)

The English reaction to *Le Cavalier seul* would probably be that it is old-fashioned rant, spiced agreeably with sex and a little grotesque humour. Yet it cannot be denied that it has a core of meaning and structure: and a dominantly suburban and lower-middle-class audience gave it a rapturous reception at the Théâtre de l'Est, where it was revived. The critic of *L'Express*, Robert Kanters, wrote:

'Avec *Le Cavalier seul*, c'est la revanche du texte, de la parole. C'est un superbe et scintillant morceau d'éloquence, une longue confrontation passionnée entre l'Occident et l'Orient.... Audiberti ne tarit jamais: sur l'homme, sur la femme, sur la guerre, sur l'amour, sur la nature, il a toujours un couplet brillant à entonner. Le chevalier Mirtus part pour s'agenouiller devant le Tombeau de Jérusalem, Audiberti est parti pour démontrer que ce tombeau est vide, et vain le christianisme. Mirtus pariera pour l'homme, l'homme complet, l'homme païen, mais il rencontrera, cependant, le fils de l'homme, ou son ombre, et l'acteur qui tient le rôle (Pierre Tabard) lui donne tant de force que la mythologie chrétienne ne semble pas tout a fait vaincue.'

(*L'Express*, 6.8.73)

(With *Le Cavalier seul*, we see the text and the word taking its revenge ... it's a superb and scintillating slice of eloquence, a long and passionate confrontation between East and West ... Audiberti never stops on man, woman, war, love, nature, there's always a brilliant and sonorous flourish. The knight Mirtus sets out to kneel before the Holy Sepulchre in Jerusalem; Audiberti sets out to show the tomb is empty, and Christianity's a sham. Mirtus will go on backing man, the whole man, pagan man, but he's due to meet the son of man, or his double, while the actor who plays him (Pierre Tabard) brings such force that Christian mythology doesn't seem beaten at all.)

PAUL CLAUDEL (1868–1955) is an often derided figure, yet he is undoubtedly, and will remain, one of the few great poets and dramatists of his day. The English critic, George Steiner, ranks him equal to Brecht: 'Claudel is a maddening writer: he is pompous, intolerant, rhetorical, amateurish, prolix—what you will. Many of his plays are fantastically turgid, and there are in all of them patches of arid vehemence. He stomps through the theatre like an incensed bull, goring and tossing and finally running into the wall with a great crack of horns. But no matter. There is enough grandeur left, enough sheer power of invention, to make Claudel one of the two great lyric playwrights of the century.' For Jean-Louis Barrault, the greatest living French actor, he is a father figure: Claudel once defined the 'word' for him as an 'intelligible mouthful', and Barrault never found a better definition. Antonin Artaud was responsible for putting on the first act of *Partage de midi* (Division of Noon, 1905) but it was Barrault who became so enthusiastic over presenting his works that he virtually based his post-Second World War reputation at the Marigny, and later at the Odéon, on their success. Barrault has described how he went to see Claudel in 1939 when his wife, Madeleine Renaud, was about to play in Claudel's *L'Annonce faite à. Marie* (The Tidings brought to Mary, 1909) at the Comédie-Française, and asked Claudel's permission to put on *Tête d'or* (Head of Gold, 1889), *Partage de midi*, and *Le Soulier de satin* (The Satin

Slipper, 1929). Claudel asked him why he wanted to put on these three hitherto unperformed plays, and Barrault replied 'Because *Tête d'or* is your sap, *Partage* is your ordeal, and the *Soulier* your epitome.'

Claudel's plays were written over a very long period, and, like Brecht's, they were subject to meticulous and ruthless revision by the author. He became converted to Catholicism at the age of eighteen, and his early work contains much of the symbolism fashionable at the time, though the general direction is away from this and towards the more formal concerns of sin and redemption through God's grace. The first version of *Tête d'or* was written as far back as 1889; it is a heroic, powerful play of conquest 'in between Aeschylus, Nietzsche, paganism, and conversion.' Claudel forbade its performance for religious reasons during his own lifetime, but Barrault presented it to open the Odéon-Théâtre de France in 1959, and it became a landmark in post-war French theatre, although rarely playing to audiences of more than 50 per cent.

The other major theatrical event of the Occupation besides Anouilh's *Antigone* was the first production of *Le Soulier de satin* in 1943, also by Barrault. Written between 1922 and 1924, and published in 1929, *Le Soulier* is also a monumental play, and it takes place over four days. As the critic Alfred Simon has written, 'it mixes up periods, covers continents, unites heaven and earth, the visible and the invisible, and, in a great burst of total theatre, answers, in Claudel's own words, the question put in *Partage de midi*: the reciprocal role of sin and grace in the ordering of providence.' Into the production of *Le Soulier*, Barrault was able to put 'the whole works: mime (the waves), nudity (the negress), madness, order/disorder alternating, to the advantage not of reason but of imagination.' The result was that Claudel gained a popularity with the general as opposed to the Catholic public which had always followed his poetry: he was never to lose it again. General de Gaulle commented after the revival in 1959: 'Ce Claudel, tout de même, il a du ragoût.' (That Claudel, when all is said, has got some spice.)

Partage de midi is about an ordeal which Claudel suffered so deeply that its effects were with him all his life. He wrote it after a ten year silence. Mesa has suffered a set-back in his desire to take the holy vow, and in leaving France and travelling to the Orient he falls headlong in love with Ysé, a married woman. *Partage* can be seen as a debate between the spirit and the flesh, or a hymn to earthly love; either way, Claudel created a pair of lovers to rank beside the greatest of all time.

In their final climactic scene, in an ecstasy of contrition, meeting on what Steiner has called the 'rim of death', Claudel's style is shown at its most pure and eloquent:

Ysé apparaît au fond inondée de lumière de lune, comme immatérielle. Sans la voir.

MESA: Moi, c'est cela que j'ai tiré au sort, c'est cela que j'ai gagné, cette sacrée loterie qui ne cesse pas un moment de se combiner et de se recombiner.

Moi, c'est cela que j'ai tiré au sort.

(*Il crie fort commes s'il appelait.*)

Cette personne inexplicablement, cette âme détestablement pour que je m'y procure, dans cette âme, comme je peux, la clef de la mienne.

YSÉ: Qu'est-ce qui parle?

Je dis: qui est-ce qui parle derrière moi dans la nuit, qu'on ne voit pas?

YSÉ: Mesa, je suis Ysé, c'est moi.

MESA: Partez. Il n'y a plus de temps à perdre.

Vous savez bien ce qui va arriver.

YSÉ: Vous pensez bien que les Chinois n'avaient pas le temps. C'était le courant, à toute vitesse, qui emportait la barque. Je n'ai entendu qu'un cri dans la nuit, une espèce de cri ridicule.

MESA: Est-ce que je rêve encore?

YSÉ: Les rêves sont finis, Mesa, il n'y a plus que la vérité.

MESA: Mesa, je suis Ysé, c'est moi.

Mesa, je suis Ysé, c'est moi.

YSÉ: Et dire que c'est ça que j'ai aimé. Pauvre Ysé!

MESA: Et moi je ne dis plus pauvre Mesa.

YSÉ: Tout de même, il n'a pas réussi à s'en débarrasser de cette Ysé. Ce n'est pas aussi commode que ça de s'en débarrasser de cette personne.

MESA: Me voici les membres rompus comme un criminel sur la roue, et toi, l'âme outrée, sortie de ton corps comme une épée à demi dégainée.

(*Ysé appears in the distance bathed in moonlight, as if incorporeal. Without seeing him.*)

YSÉ: I'm what I've drawn from fate. I'm what I've won, in that sacred lottery, which never stops a moment combining and recombining its numbers.

I'm what I've drawn from fate.

(*shouts as if calling*)

The person inexplicably, the soul detestably, though I may procure there, in that soul, as best I can, the key to my own.

YSÉ: A catch!

MESA: Who is it?

I say: who's speaking behind me in the night, who can't be seen.

YSÉ: Mesa, I'm Ysé, it's me.

MESA: Go. There's no time to lose. You know what's going to happen.

YSÉ: You were right in thinking the Chinese wouldn't have time.

It was the current, at full speed, which carried their boat away. All I heard was a shout in the night; a kind of ridiculous shout.

MESA: Am I still dreaming?

YSÉ: Dreams are over, Mesa, there's only truth now.

MESA: Mesa, I'm Ysé, it's me.

Mesa, I'm Ysé, it's me.

YSÉ: And to say that's what I loved. Poor Ysé.

MESA: And now I no longer say poor Mesa.

YSÉ: All the same, he hasn't succeeded in getting rid of that Ysé. It's not as easy as you think to get rid of that person.

MESA: Look at my limbs broken like a criminal on the wheel, and you, outraged soul, sticking out from your body like a half-drawn sword.)

Beside the three most monumental expressions of Claudel's genius *Protée* (Proteus, 1913) is a slight work, but the enthusiastic reception which greeted its revival shows the esteem in which Claudel is still held.

Proteus was a prophetic old man of the sea, a kind of sacred king, buried on a coastal island, who took various shapes such as a fish, a lion and a stag. In Claudel's play he remains an old man throughout, and, following the legend as told by Homer in Book IV of *The Odyssey*, Menelaus and Helen land on the island on their way home after the sack of Troy. In a '*Tempest*-like' plot, aided by a seductive nymph called Brindosier, they try to dislodge Proteus from the throne of his island. What emerged from the recent production was the absurdist element, underlined by the use of the original music Darius Milhaud wrote—haunting, melodic evocations of primitive godlike and sea-animal sounds, conch-shells with succulently rich vibrations. The way Helen is led by Menelaus on to the stage in the first scene, in chains, wearing sun-glasses, while Menelaus sports tropical kit, is strongly reminiscent of Pozzo and Lucky's first entrance in *Waiting for Godot*.

Barrault has said of Claudel that of 'all the masters we have chosen to play, Claudel is the most nourishing, the most generative influence.' His plays have been most influential in their anti-naturalistic spirit, their emphasis on the game-playing and witty aspects of theatrical art: like Shakespeare and Molière, they invite continual new production in changing fashions and tastes, and Claudel is one of the first of contemporary playwrights that directors have found suitable to experiment with. Barrault began his first season at the Odéon in 1959 with *Tête d'or*, while Jorge Lavelli, a noted and gifted director in more adventurous venues, did a revolutionary production of *L'Echange* in 1967. In *L'Echange* (The Exchange, 1893) four characters, each incarnating a primordial essence, are juggled in a game of life and death.

As well as Audiberti and Claudel, JEAN GIRAUDOUX (1882–1944) is an important figure. His plays are constantly revived, and, as far as French audiences are concerned, have stood the test of time. The reverse would appear to be the case with Jean Cocteau (1889–1963) whose great versatility in all forms especially the film and the ballet has detracted from his lasting influence as a playwright. *Les Monstres sacrés* (The Holy Terrors, 1940), a melodrama about life in the theatre, the romantic *L'Aigle à deux têtes* (The Eagle has Two Heads, 1946), or the even more profound *Les Parents terribles* (Intimate Relations, 1946), are marked more by anti-naturalistic eclecticism than by originality. But Cocteau was an innovator with Greek myth, and his *Antigone* (1922) and *La Machine infernale* (Infernal Machine, 1934) paved the way for the wartime use of myth by Anouilh and Sartre.

Three new plays by Giraudoux were first staged after his death: *La Folle de Chaillot* (The Madwoman of Chaillot, 1945), *L'Apollon de Bellac* (The Apollo of Bellac, 1947) and *Pour Lucrèce* (For Lucretia, 1953). When Sartre, Brecht, and then Beckett were discovered in the fifties and sixties by Parisian audiences, Giraudoux's reputation suffered a temporary eclipse. But in 1962 *La Guerre de Troie n'aura pas lieu* (The Trojan War Will Not Take Place, 1935) was triumphantly revived by Jean Vilar in the open air at Avignon, and then, three years later, *La Folle de Chaillot* really came into its own, when it was performed at the TNP with Edwige Feuillère in the leading role. The irony of *La Folle de Chaillot*, the tone of denunciation, the savage juxtaposition of the past view, in the person of La Folle and La Môme Bijou, with the present reality of big business and property speculation destroying the traditional beauty of Paris, by then had all the more relevance. Giraudoux's treatment of the theme is not social, but fanciful, surreal in image, brilliant in verbal invention.

Giraudoux not only embodies the literary tradition in his own works, but he is its best exponent. In *L'Impromptu de Paris* (1937) a fascinating dialogue between well-known theatrical personalities of the time dominated by Louis Jouvet (1887–1951) whose own career as a director embraced Cocteau, Giraudoux, Sartre, and Genet, many aspects of the theatre are discussed ('the greatest of the arts' one of the personalities insists).

The debate in *L'Impromptu* is witty and acute. Bouquet-Robineau, for example, asks Jouvet if there are some critics who don't think like him; Jouvet's reply is, characteristically: 'Yes. Those are the bad critics.' The belief in the word, in the literary value of the text, is profound, and sustained throughout with every ounce of passion and intellect Giraudoux can summon behind it. For the actor, Boverio asks 'will you tell me what will become of the actor, sir, if there is any other honour besides that of language and style?' As for the critics, Jouvet attacks them by saying 'if the French stage has for decades been a refuge for puppets and stereotypes, if the dramatic language hasn't gone further than dialect, if the French theatre has fallen gravely short of its nobility, which is the word, and in its honour, which is truth, then they are the first we must hold responsible.' This view is endorsed by Jean-Louis Barrault, who in 1960 writes:

'The critics, for the last ten years, bear a heavy responsibility for the disarray now prevailing in our theatres. Artists and members of audiences—from avant-garde extremists to immobilist conservatives—no longer known to which saints they should turn.'

But the best expression and defence of the literary theatre in *L'Impromptu* comes not from Jouvet himself but from the actor Bogar who tries to explain Jouvet's more impassioned utterances to the others:

'What Jouvet wants to say is that the theatre is not a theorem, but an entertainment ('spectacle'), not a lesson, but a filter. That it has less to enter your spirit than your imagination and your sense, and it is for this, in my opinion, that the talent for writing is indispensable, for it is the style which reflects on the audience's soul a thou-

sand shafts of light, a thousand iridescences which they have no
more need to understand than motes of sunlight glancing off a
mirror.'

The Influence of Brecht

The influence of Bertold Brecht (1898–1956) has been very considerable on recent French theatre; certain key directors, such as
Vilar, Planchon, Rétoré, have been enormously conditioned by his
plays and theoretical writings, and many of the playwrights who
have come to the fore since the war have been fervent Brechtians (see
Chapter 9). The idea of a popular theatre, realized largely in Vilar's
dual creations of the Avignon Festival and of the Théâtre National
Populaire (TNP), Vilar set down in his book *De la Tradition
théâtrale*. Brecht himself wrote in *Petit Organum pour le théâtre*
(L'Arche, 1948).

> 'Let's suppose there weren't other reasons, but just on its own the
> desire to develop our art to conform to the needs of our age is
> sufficient motive to push our theatre of the scientific age out to the
> suburbs, where, as if open to all winds, it's at the disposal of those
> who produce a lot and live badly, in order to permit them to amuse
> themselves usefully with their important problems ... we must
> learn and discover their needs, and the best means of responding
> to them. . . .'

While echoing him in many ways Vilar added 'It must be realized
that the theatre is not only an entertainment, it isn't an object of
luxury, but an overriding need in all men and women.'

Brecht has described going into a theatre and watching the effects
of a play on the audience. 'Immobile silhouettes, plunged into a
strange state ... eyes wide open, but looking at nothing: just fixed ...
the expression comes from the Middle Ages, from the time of priests
and witches. To look and to listen means to be active.' Vilar, who
exemplified the practical man of the theatre, wrote 'We must strip
away everything.' Of American theatre Vilar wrote 'they're afraid,
there, of the speech, and of the word. They cling to an utterly
realistic, crude form of dialogue, a kind of stenographer's shorthand.'
Then follows an important phrase, 'On évite la prise de conscience
des personnages.'

'Prise de conscience': does there exist an English equivalent?
Moral stocktaking? Moment of truth? Sartre says roughly the same
thing as Vilar when he talks about Anglo-Saxon theatre consisting
largely of stories of 'defeat, *laissez-faire*, and drifting'.

That an insignificant Brecht play should have been successfully
revived in 1973 shows not only how popular Brecht is with the
younger playgoing public (something which is only recently
happening in England), but also how French companies have gone
through the established works, and are falling back on the early for-
mative pieces. Anti-fascism always goes over well in continental
Europe, but the interesting element in the revival of *La Noce chez les
petits bourgeois* (Originally *Die Hochzeit*, The Wedding, 1923) is
how the Theatre of the Absurd is now itself an influence on the

present-day treatment of Brecht. The whole play is turned into an anti-totalitarian satire on the rise of Nazism in the same way *The Resistible Rise of Arturo Ui* is a satire on Hitler, whereas Brecht intended merely a mild skit on the middle classes. Although the wedding party is treated with the now familiar tricks of the absurd—furniture which collapses under guests, a pregnant bride, a cumulative revelation of skeletons in the cupboard—it is the reactionary spirit of the party which was brought to the forefront in the Compagnie Vincent-Jourdheuil's production. One sees this anti-reactionary spirit very much at work in many of the younger, or more recent playwrights: in Armand Gatti, in *Deux Chants pour les chaises électriques* (Two Songs for Electric Chairs, 1966) and *V comme Vietnam* (1967); also in Victor Haïm, in Philip Adrien, in Marguerite Duras' *Suzanna Andler*, which has been seen in London, in J. L. Grumberg, in René Ehni, and in the work of directors like Planchon or Ariane Mnouchkine who either write or originate their own productions as a collective venture.

Brecht's influence is very strong not only in its dissemination of anti-totalitarian attitudes, which made such of his works as *Antigone* and *The Visions of Simone Machard* popular, but also in its anti-psychological impact. Characters in Brecht's plays are not meant to be real people for which we form sentimental, personal attachments. Imaginative sympathy is often accompanied by physical stillness, and in his description of a bourgeois audience, quoted above, Brecht fails to see how one is consequent upon the other. Brecht has, in addition, a horror of conformity and obedience, thinking it automatically Fascist, which may be true of Germany when he grew up, but is not necessarily true of other periods or other countries. In his continual war against what was personal and individual (a war one does not actually find in some of those he has influenced, such as Jean Vilar, whose love of the heroic and comic bourgeois classics remained steadfast), his theory of 'alienation' arose. This is known in France as 'distanciation'.

'The spectator must always be able to interpose his own judgement', he wrote. This is the very opposite of the 'suspension of disbelief' which most bourgeois theatre attempts to achieve. Still, alienation is a puritan observance most honoured in the breach, and good productions of Brecht have a capacity to sweep away critical reserve as strongly as in any classically bourgeois play. But alienation has retained such a strong theoretical attraction for French writers that it is fashionable for them to despise any popular success their plays might achieve in the commercial bourgeois theatre. Jean-Paul Sartre is an example of this.

The Influence of Artaud

'Surrealism has opened up a field of vision limited only by the mind's capacity for nervous excitement. It goes without saying that this has been a great blow to the critics, who are terrified to see the author's importance being reduced to a minimum and the conception of talent abolished' wrote Max Ernst. To talk about the 'influence of Artaud' is a convenient way of describing all those factors in the French theatre of today which are broadly 'surreal' in spirit. Sartre, who belongs to the other school, would call them bourgeois because he sees logic and intelligence, traditional elements however left-wing and revolutionary in purpose, as being in opposition to the human qualities of the absurdist writers, their essential loneliness, despair and obsession with non-communication, and to the pure surrealists, who delight in an anarchy and chaos which is ultimately un-questioning and reassuring to the middle classes. Akin to surrealism in painting was, of course, the dada movement in painting and poetry, and some of the formulas of dadaism became popular again after the student uprising in 1968, like 'art is dead', or Apollinaire's 'we are all poets'.

Guillaume Apollinaire's own play. *Les Mamelles de Tirésias* (The Breasts of Tiresias, 1917) is a notable forerunner of the surrealist movement in the theatre, together with Alfred Jarry's timeless creations, some twenty years earlier, of *Ubu roi, Ubu cocu, Ubu enchaîné,* and *Ubu sur la butte* (Ubu King, Cuckold, In Chains, Bumped Off, 1896 onwards). Apollinaire was responsible for inventing the phrase 'drame surréaliste', and *Les Mamelles de Tirésias* is a burlesque treatment of the theme of sexuality, when Thérèse, refusing her conjugal role, strips off the red and white balloons which serve her as breasts, and becomes Tiresias. The Ubu character was based originally on a parody of *Macbeth* and at the famous first performance of *Ubu roi*, on 10 December 1896, the audience included Yeats, Mallarmé, and Jacques Copeau, who was seventeen. The sequence was revived, in a triumphant production by Jean Vilar, at the TNP in 1958.

ANTONIN ARTAUD (1896–1948) stresses the fragility of performance, but also its supremacy. Production must be considered as a 'language in space and movement.' It must always be 'subject to caution, to revision' so that if a spectator returns after several days he will not see the same performance twice.

Peter Brook and Charles Marowiz explored Artaud's idea of cruelty in their Theatre of Cruelty season at LAMDA in London, where Artaud's own play *The Spurt of Blood* was staged. The Theatre of Cruelty stems not only from an aesthetic need to find deeper and subconscious means to awaken the buried sensibilities of the spectator, these means often being more brutally direct (lights, unexpected noise, violent gesture, etc.) than the conventionally structured play, but also from a deeply moral concern with the nature of good and evil. In a little known and remarkable passage Artaud has spoken of this in a letter to Jean Paulhan, written in 1932:

'I use the word cruelty in the sense of life appetite, cosmic rigour and implacable necessity, in the gnostic sense of a whirlwind which devours the shadows, in the sense of that pain outside of whose ineluctable necessity life cannot be lived; good is willed, evil is permanent. The hidden god, when he created, obeyed the cruel necessity of the creation he imposed on himself, and he could *not* not create, could *not* not admit to the centre of the voluntary whirlwind of good, a kernel of evil more and more reduced, more and more eaten away. And the theatre in the sense of continual creation, of entire magical action obeys that necessity. A play without that will, that blind appetite for life, which is capable of passing over everything, visible in each gesture, in each action, and in the side which transcends action, is a useless and failed play.'

Curiously enough it is the American Living Theatre which has most literally followed Artaud's teachings, while his influence on his own countrymen, like Genet, like the left-wing Gatti, has been more subtly assimilated. Gatti has benefited from the scenic freedom while trying to maintain a political lucidity. Artaud's influence on the more formal exiles who have been grouped together as playwrights of the absurd is a more intellectual one. They have maintained the supremacy of the work but introduced shock tactics into its treatment (see Chapters 5 and 6). But, necessarily, in a philosophy of the theatre which proclaims the supremacy of the production over all else the greatest influence Artaud has had is over directors: this has been most directly transmitted into the most recent French theatre by the Living Theatre productions.

There are three main ones: *Mysteries and Smaller Pieces, Paradise Now*, and Brecht's *Antigone*, all first performed in Paris. The first is a series of controlled Artaud-esque exercises: one example is an actor standing still on the stage for over seven minutes without a word being spoken, in order to provoke the audience. (Peter Handke's *Offending the Audience* was written later.) This provocation is followed up more directly in *Antigone* where the actors spill out violently over the audience, hissing and threatening, and in *Paradise Now*, where they whisper into the ears of individual members sentences of futility and frustration against the banks, authority and the conformity of society. There is virtually no text in *Antigone* and what few lines remain are chanted and repeated over and over again, like 'he who has no enemy becomes his own enemy.' In *Paradise Now* is a phrase in which their theatre is seen, for all its gaucheness and ill-discipline, to aspire to the most exalted notions of Artaud: 'To get to know God in his madness.'

A belief in the holiness of the theatre, which its prophet Artaud left behind him as potent, mysterious, and unfinished as his own existence which tailed off into madness, has permeated all sides of the theatre, and all shades of its participants, endowing and sustaining the theatre's power to transmit experience with oracular force.

3 Theatre of choice (I)

> '... these Jesuits who were the masters of our friends the com-
> munists ...'
>
> J.-P. Sartre

The French assume rottennes in their body politic; they assume corruption, governmental bias in Government-run broadcasting
networks, bribery in the police, and scandal in high places. However
much they dislike it, they assume that, to some extent, the exercise of
power is a dirty business. When they refer to 'perfide Albion' more
often than not they mean English hypocrisy; the example of Lord
Cromer who, before England devalued the pound during the Wilson
1964–70 Government, appeared on French television as Governor of
the Bank of England and stated that on no account would England
devalue the pound, has been pointed out many times. What annoyed
the French was that they believed him.

The French also assume their police are rough, as one saw in the
student riots of 1968, when the outcry provoked by the violence of
the C.R.S., a para-military police organization formed for the protec-
tion of the State against its enemies, was quickly stifled. That the law
ought to, and can, be gentle and applied reasonably is an Anglo-
Saxon luxury when compared to the practice of most European countries. But French political life is not only compounded, as in most
places, of brutality, bribery, and corruption, but also of paradox, skill,
and intelligence. The student protestors who were so vociferous
against their C.R.S. assailants were, in 1968, too young to know that
seven or eight years previously the same C.R.S. were laying just as
heavily into the ferocious revolutionaries of the right, the O.A.S. and
the Algérie Française movement. Instead of Danny Cohn-Bendit it
was the right-wing student Pierre Lagaillarde whose name was on
everyone's lips. In 1968 the students might have felt emotionally, for
a day or two, that they had De Gaulle's Fifth Republic tottering, but
in that crop of uprisings between 1959 and 1962 the activists of the
right were far nearer, led by fanatics such as Joseph Ortiz and backed
by a sizable proportion of the French army and élite corps, to
shattering the precarious and never very satisfactory balance of the
French democratic process. It was then the young men of student age
(the same as those in 1968 who were tearing up cobblestones and
manning the barricades), drafted into the army in Algeria as con-
scripts, who remained loyal to De Gaulle. In that era the C.R.S. were
much loved and honoured, and cheered by Moslem crowds in the
streets of Algiers for their impartiality.

Communism has been an openly accepted fact among the politically aware French working class for many a decade. The self-conscious

Marxism of some English writers who confuse their own personal alienation and disgust with general corruption and decline, as if relishing their love of apocalypse, is absent. It would, in France, probably be considered naïve. As Louis-Ferdinand Céline far-sightedly wrote in his play *L'Eglise* (The Church) in 1933, 'if you're intelligent, don't stay in France, go to ... New York; here, the intelligent proletariat become revolutionaries; over there they sometimes make a fortune.'

The State has a finger in everything in France including the theatre; foreigners to France, especially the British, are unaware that an elephantine share of French industry is owned by the nation: Air France, Renault, the main banks, insurance companies, mines, even transport, aeronautical, and tobacco companies, are all State-owned. Nationalization may be an inefficient bogey in England, but in France it is (or was, till the time of writing!) to some degree responsible for the fastest and most efficient growth-rate in Europe, and a public-spirited relationship between Government and industry which has been the envy of Europe. The educational system is far more competitively centralized, and therefore the managers, who are openly an élite cadre, are far more interrelated even than in England, where the old school tie results in much inward-looking parochialism.

The managerial centralization in France is one of intellectual ability, uncluttered by sentimental notions of educational and anti-competitive equality. If there is one thing the French are not interested in, it is levelling everyone out. The State can call upon the wealth of talent and experience of its foremost intellectuals in a way that is inconceivable in England. President Pompidou, who was himself a frequent visitor to the theatre, was formerly a banker in the Rothschild bank; Jean Giraudoux was an Under-Secretary of State in the Daladier government in 1942, and the former, highly successful Minister of Culture, André Malraux, is still a distinguished man of letters. That a politician should be responsible for culture in France is quite unthinkable.

In the theatre, intellectuals like Sartre have been politically active over subjects such as Vietnam (in the way the ageing Trotskyist in Trevor Griffiths' *The Party* tells his friends they should become involved in the Third World). There have been a far larger number of politically engaged plays, not only on Vietnam, but on the Congo, the situation of foreign workers in France, the evils of foreign dictators like General Franco. In 1969, for example, Armand Gatti's play on Franco, *Passion en violet, jaune et rouge* (Passion in Violet, Yellow and Red) was forbidden production by the Minister of the Interior: censorship in France still has teeth, though its abolition in the future has now been announced.

But if communism has been an openly accepted part of French political life for a long time, and labour relations between managements and workers appear to be better than in England (though one potentially theatrical device in French industrial strife has yet to be introduced into England, the locking up of managers in their own factories), one has also to remember that the right-wing is also intellectually respectable and credible. Figures such as Céline, whose *L'Eglise* was recently revived, or Claudel, as well as Montherlant, enjoy the highest possible esteem. Two of the biggest successes of recent years have been Montherlant's *La Ville dont le prince est un enfant* (The Town in which the Prince is a Child, 1951) and *Port-Royal* (1954).

Marxist art enjoys in France a very different status from what it does in England or America. The music critic Andrew Porter summarized the Anglo-Saxon paradox when he wrote of Hans Werner Henze in the *Financial Times*, 'Henze is the leading socialist artist of our day. Ever since that fiery Marxist declaration he published on the eve of the first performance of his Second Piano Concerto five years ago, he has been working out, in music, the problems of a committed socialist composer fêted and fussed over by the capitalists who constitute his audience, provide his livelihood, and like his music.'

It is probably another Anglo-Saxon luxury to suffer criticism and remain unchanged. Marxist playwrights in France do not seem to write for commercial films or television series as do their English or American counterparts: they work at other jobs and write in their spare time. Their work is not a fantasy-castigation enjoyed by their patrons. In France they are neither persecuted nor martyred, nor are they especially tolerated. When in 1970 the, by then ageing, Marxist-theorist playwright Arthur Adamov committed suicide he was as poor as when he started out, or probably even poorer for he was, as Martin Esslin tells us in *The Theatre of the Absurd*, the son of a wealthy oil-proprietor of Armenian origin. No Wednesday Play for Arthur Adamov! The Minister of Culture, Maurice Druon, who succeeded Jacques Duhamel in April 1973, provoked a very strong reaction when he said that those who came begging at his door with a hat in one hand and a Molotov cocktail in the other would have to choose.

It is only Sartre's intellectual depth and experience which makes him a great playwright: not any depth of sensibility, nor passion, nor sense of realism, except for journalistic everyday realism in current affairs and *real-politik*. He is the perfect example of the schematic, man-of-ideas writer who in the last act is desperately trying to force his characters round to fit his thesis. As George Steiner has written, 'like Diderot, Sartre and Camus make of dramatic action a parable of philosophic or political argument. The theatrical form is nearly fortuitous; the plays are essays or pamphlets declaimed and underlined by graphic gesture. In these allegories we hear voices, not characters.' As he has said himself, he has no psychology: 'psychology is a waste of time in the theatre because plays are long.' This kind of statement shows both Sartre's strength and his weakness: strength, because his drama, as his life, is concerned with the exercise of will; weakness, because human understanding and what one might broadly call religious compassion, are conspicuously absent.

Sartre was awarded the Nobel prize in 1954, but his dramatic output since then has been slight. His early and influential plays like *Huis clos* (In Camera, 1943) *Les Mains sales* (Dirty Hands, 1948) and *Les Mouches* (The Flies, 1947) are violent and centred round a single event. He sets himself to practise an almost classic simplicity, and uses language with a rigorous sense of economy ('the moment it ceases dealing with action, it is boring').

Theatre is where we find the representation of action. 'Sculpture represents the form of the body; the theatre represents the act of the body.' But he wants action in the theatre to be objective with all the clarity of philosophical exactness, not in the sense that Brecht sought an epic clarity ('the ideal of Brechtian theatre would be if the public became a group of ethnographers suddenly meeting a small tribe of savage people. Going up to them and saying, stupified: 'savages? they're us'), but in a form where motives and consequences of action can be seen and comprehended in all their significance. He does not abolish the complex individual hero. Paradoxically, in trying to free him from the false trappings of his individuality, he asserts his value. His individuals are all very passionate: 'the impassioned man is much less stupid than is generally believed; on the contrary he's a type who is trying to see with the greatest lucidity. What are his limits? His right: he doesn't go beyond his right.' Although Sartre has denounced any future individual role for the writer, claiming that the writer's role will be to participate continually in the collective work of the troupe (mistakenly, for brilliant troupes like Ariane Mnouchkine's Théâtre du Soleil have no need of writers at all), his own achievement has been that of reviving some of the pomp and ceremony of Greek drama in modern, ideological and existential conflict. In an essay on Jean Giraudoux (1940) Sartre insists that, in order to enter into Giraudoux's universe of pure Aristotelian forms, one must forget one's own genuine experience of reality, 'this soft, unstable paste, shot through by waves which have their origin elsewhere'.

His own attempts, however, at using Greek mythology in *Les Mouches*, and in his version of Euripides' *Les Troyennes* (The Trojan Women, 1965), are less successful than Giraudoux's and Anouilh's, the latter especially in *Antigone* (1941), where the use of myth was a kind of secret code used in defiance of the Nazi conqueror.

On 3 June 1943, with permission of the German censorship authorities, Jean-Paul Sartre's first play was produced by Charles Dullin's company at the Théâtre de la Cité in Paris. Sartre chose to base his play on a Greek legend for several reasons. First, he had been teaching Greek tragedy to Dullin's pupils. Second, the work of Giraudoux, in particular *La Guerre de Troie n'aura pas lieu*, had accustomed French audiences to seeing contemporary events in plays based on classical antiquity. Sartre wanted to show how a man could take responsibility for a crime, even though it filled him with horror. If he had made up a situation in which a man killed his mother it would have seemed too rare a happening to cause much identification among his audience: mythology provided the answer. Moreover, traditional insistence on the importance of fatality as the force behind Orestes' action allowed Sartre, by contrast, to emphasize the strength of liberty.

Les Mouches opens with the arrival of Orestes and his tutor at Argos. The only living things seem to be the flies which buzz incessantly. A mysterious traveller who has been following Orestes and the tutor for some time explains that the inhabitants of Argos are wholly taken up with expiating their guilt over the death of Agamemnon. The flies have been sent by the gods to remind the people of their guilt which they share by not having done anything to prevent the murder. Clytemnestra and Aegisthus keep their power by reminding their subjects of their share of guilt: were the subjects to recognize their innocence, the political order would collapse. After the traveller, who is Zeus in disguise, has left, Orestes complains to his tutor that he feels at home nowhere, and that even in his native city he feels a stranger. He longs to commit some action, which, even though a crime, would give him a right to live in Argos and feel part of the city.

In the second and third acts, emphasis is placed on the philosophical aspects of the play. On the Day of the Dead, when the people of Argos invite their dead relatives to return and torture them with their crimes, Electra stands up and denounces the ceremony as a fraud. Orestes tries to persuade Electra to leave Argos with him. Electra replies that she cannot leave and give up hope of her father's death being avenged. Zeus warns Orestes he ought to leave. But Orestes reflects that to do good always seems to involve acceptance and submission. Suddenly, he realizes he is free to avenge his father, and thus acquire the right to live among the people of Argos. He and Electra go to the palace; there, hiding behind a throne, they overhear Zeus warning Aegisthus of Orestes' murderous intentions. Aegisthus refuses to save himself and, when he asks Zeus why he doesn't strike Orestes down with a thunderbolt, Zeus replies that once liberty has exploded in man's soul the gods can do nothing against him. Orestes then kills Aegisthus and Clytemnestra. But as soon as the horrible deed is accomplished, Electra regrets her brother's revenge, and grows afraid of the goddesses of remorse and the furies represented by the omnipresent flies. The last act emphasizes the difference between Orestes, the man who is truly free and accepts the consequences of his action, and Electra, who cannot bring herself to accept responsibility for a crime of which she had so long dreamed. The traditional departure of Orestes fleeing from the wrath of the furies is changed by Sartre into the conscious assumption by a free man of all the consequences of his acts. He walks out of Argos drawing the flies after him.

The play was badly received in 1943 although Maurice Rostand praised it in *Paris-Soir*. The revival in 1951 didn't do much better. Even though it was not attacked politically, legend has it that Alain Lambreaux, critic of the anti-semitic *Je Suis Partout*, brought a number of thugs with him to try to break up the performance, and there is a picturesque story to the effect that he and Sartre fought each other with long cudgels during the intervals. The Communists reacted equally strongly when the play was put on at the Nîmes Festival in 1950. Gallimard published a text shortly after the first performance, and most critics agreed the play was better read. Giving an old story new meaning obviously necessitates explanation but Sartre has not Shaw's talent for making long speeches interesting through irony or paradox, nor Giraudoux's capacity for remaining detached.

Sartre's other attempt at mythology is recent, and also relates to war, this time the war in Algeria. The action of *Les Troyennes* takes place by the walls of defeated Troy. It follows Euripides closely. The victorious Greeks are preparing to return home, taking with them the captive wives of Priam and Hector (Hecuba and Andromache), and Cassandra, the daughter of Priam. It opens with Poseidon declaring his anger with the Greeks for insulting him; in Scene II, Poseidon persuades his former enemy, Pallas Athene, to help him in making the victors pay for their lack of respect to the Gods.

The rest of *Les Troyennes*, as in Euripides, centres round Hecuba as she grieves over the downfall of Troy and the consequent loss of husband and sons. In two scenes she tries to curb, first, the mad ravings of Cassandra who dreams how, once forced into marriage with Agamemnon, she will make his life hell.

Who wants to embrace the daughter of the sun
Will never see light again.
Endless night will devour you;

Next, Hecuba tries to persuade her daughter-in-law, Andromache, to save her son by becoming the mistress of the Greek Neoptolemus, the son of the man who killed her husband Hector. Andromache is contemptuous of Hecuba's suggestion and horrified she could think of defiling her son's memory in such a way. Andromache stoically accepts the inevitability of her son's death. This provides one of the most moving scenes of the play: her son is dropped like a stone from a high tower. In the last scene Hecuba is confronted by Helen, whom she admonishes for being the cause of the tragedy. Helen defends herself by saying she was the victim of Aphrodite's vanity.

Les Troyennes ends with Menelaus carrying Hecuba off back to Greece while Poseidon promises to avenge her; in the last lines, Poseidon cries in warning to all mortals against the futility of war:

Idiots.
We'll make you pay for this.
You stupid bestial mortals
Making war, burning cities,
Violating tombs and temples,
Torturing your enemies,
Bringing suffering on yourselves
Can't you see
War
Will kill you:
All of you?

In his preface, Sartre states that *Les Troyennes* came to his notice during the Algerian War in a very faithful translation by Jacqueline Moatti. He saw in it an explicit condemnation of war in general, and of colonial war in particular. 'We know today that war would trigger off an atomic war in which there would be neither victor nor vanquished. This play demonstrates this fact precisely: that war is a defeat to humanity.' The Greeks destroy Troy, but they receive no benefit for their victory. The gods punish their belligerence by making them perish themselves.

Another theme from Euripides emphasized in Sartre's adaptation,

which he calls more of an 'oratorio' than a tragedy, is the plight of the
oppressed woman. Andromache's

> But I am a woman
> And a woman is only a woman
> They say it only takes just one night of
>   pleasure to master her:
> A woman is only an animal

might be Simone de Beauvoir talking. All the Trojan women feel
themselves powerless against the will of men. Andromache describes
how doing her duty as a wife and mother has worked to her disadvan-
tage, for now she finds herself unable to disregard that duty and save
herself and her child. Yet at the same time the women are not
depicted as heroic characters: there is a tone of cynicism. Hecuba
says to Menelaus when warning him against falling in love with her
again: 'Women like to keep their beauty because life doesn't touch
them. They're indifferent to the misery they cause.'

Sartre's best play is *Les Mains sales*, usually performed in English
under the title *Crime Passionel*. Like *Twelfth Night* it is set in
'Illyria'. There are seven scenes, each forming a tableau in which are
revealed the motives behind Hugo Barrine's assassination of his
party leader, Hoederer. The play opens with Hugo, who is a young
intellectual of the 'Proletarian' party, returning to headquarters after
his release from prison in 1945. There he finds Olga, a party worker,
who succeeds in securing three hours of grace for him before the
other leaders of the party come to kill him. During these three hours
Olga hopes to discover exactly why Hugo killed Hoederer, and
whether his attitude to his crime will make him useful to the party: to
use the words Sartre uses, whether he is 'fit for salvage.'

The six central scenes deal with the crime itself, its background, its
execution, the misunderstood jealousy of Hugo towards Hoederer
over his wife, Jessica, and the rules and nature of political deception
and realism. Hoederer is a truly remarkable man, prepared, as he
himself says, to get his hands dirty if it means saving thousands of
lives. He criticizes Hugo for demanding that the party should satisfy
his obsession for complete purity. Lies are inevitable. When he learns
of Hugo's mission to kill him, he confronts him with this knowledge.
But only the belief that Hoederer wants to sleep with his wife spurs
Hugo in the end to accomplish the crime.

The final scene returns to 1945, with Hugo finishing his explanation. He still cannot rationally explain why he killed Hoederer. Was it
really jealousy, or was the jealousy an emotional help to carry out his
orders, orders which he could not perform in cold blood? Chance also
played a part. If he had not opened a door at a certain moment he
would not have caught his wife in Hoederer's arms.

Olga then informs Hoederer of the final irony. When Hugo was
sent to kill Hoederer, relations with the USSR had been interrupted,
and when contact was resumed, Hoederer's proposals were proved
the best in the circumstances. In exactly the same words Hoederer
used when talking to Hugo about political realism, Olga tells Hugo
that they lied to their comrades about Hoederer's death: 'because it's

not the custom to give the troops an hour by hour account of the battle.'

Hugo then suddenly understands why he killed Hoederer: because he could not accept or participate in political deception. He shouts to the gunmen that he is not 'fit for salvage' and they mow him down. By refusing to deny what he has done, and by dying because of his refusal, he is at last killing Hoederer deliberately. So in the end Hugo takes full responsibility for his actions. As Sartre has written elsewhere 'For us, man is a total enterprise in himself. And passion is part of the enterprise.'

Les Mains sales was originally called *Les Biens de ce monde*, which emphasized Hugo's problem better, namely that he was born into the wealthy middle class, and had difficulty in adapting to revolutionary activity. Sartre was reported not to be overjoyed by the middle-class audiences who thought it was anti-communist. But he has not created a better character than Hoederer, who is the ideal of a certain kind of political man of action. Completely without illusions, he knows that, in devoting his life to politics, he must give up the adolescent purity which characterizes Hugo's commitment. Lies are regrettable but inevitable if one is fighting in a society which is still divided into classes. Hugo uses politics to escape from continual self-questioning, and demands that the party should give him a sense of purpose, satisfy his ideals, and ask him to perform heroic actions which will lead to self-perfection. The conflict between these two attitudes is the central theme of the play. But unlike characters in others of Sartre's plays. *Morts sans sépulture* (Unburied Dead, 1946), for example, they are not merely mouthpieces for Sartre's ideas. Hoederer expresses a genuine love for mankind, not usually one of Sartre's strong points:

'And I love them for what they are, with all their dirty tricks and all their vices. I love their voices and their warm hands which take hold of things, and their skin, the skin of the most naked animal, and their worried look and the desperate fight which each of them keeps up against death. and anguish. For me it matters that there should be a man more or less in the world. It's precious. I can sum you up all right, my lad, you're a destroyer. You detest men because you detest yourself; your purity is like death, and the revolution you dream of isn't ours: you don't want to change the world, you want to blow it up.'

Sartre has been quoted as saying he wrote *Le Diable et le bon Dieu* (Lucifer and the Lord, 1951) as a continuation of one of the themes of *Les Mains sales*. Whereas concentration is the strong point of the latter, complexity, even diffuseness, bedevils the clarity of the former. Like Hugo Barrine, its protagonist, Goetz, is attempting to see just how much freedom he can exercise, not in a relationship with his political ideals and party, but through a relationship with God, leading him finally to question the very existence of God.

19,400 hours were spent creating the sets and constumes of *Le Diable et le bon Dieu* before it opened at the Théâtre Antoine in 1951. The preparations were so expensive, the play required so many extra characters, that the price of all seats was upped by one third (sandwiches were made available at the bar, one commentator reported, so the audience could save on dinner). It was Louis Jouvet's last production before his death, and it ran for nine months, and was revived after six months for thirty performances, when the public were solemnly warned 'the play will not be produced in Paris again for a very long time.' It was again revived very successfully, at the TNP, in late 1968 after the student uprisings of May. This revival and the Théâtre du Soleil's *1789* gave a new impetus to theatrical debate on the political and religious nature of freedom. Not only is the story of *Le Diable et le bon Dieu* over-complicated, which spoils the theme, but the anti-Christian arguments are unconvincing: for example, who is going to be surprised if Goetz fails to find faith if he only tries for a year and a day? Many saints tried for their whole lifetime. It is the fate of revolutionaries, even revolutionary saints like the Fr Morin whom Graham Greene describes in a short story *A Visit to Morin,* that 'the world accepts them.'

From a technical point of view, Sartre has been a great innovator; with *Huis clos* (translated in America as *No Exit*), he may be said to have innovated the small 'chamber' play, with two or three characters and one set, which is now a very common phenomenon, for reasons of economy if nothing else. In *Huis clos* three dead people in 'hell' are condemned to live for eternity. The statement for which *Huis clos* is well known, namely 'l'enfer, c'est les autres' (hell, is other people) admirably summarizes the atmosphere generated by this play, though it has been, Sartre claims in a postscript, misunderstood (it is 'other people that are important in ourselves and in our understanding of ourselves'). The concentration of emotion in *Huis clos* works extremely well: in many ways it is Sartre's most actable play, and he wrote it, on his own admission, for three friends none of whom he wanted to feel had the biggest part; thus he deliberately constructed the piece so that no one could leave the set.

Sartre's longest, and in many ways most ambitious play, *Les Séquestrés d'Altona* (Altona, 1958), has much in common with *Huis clos.* Instead of three people shut up together in one place, there is a family locked together in the past, and in this family the three points of focus are on two brothers, and the youngest brother's wife.

The complicated events which make up the plot are set in motion by Von Gerlach, a rich German shipbuilder, calling his family together to tell them he has only six months to live, as he has cancer of the throat. Before he dies he wants to make his second son promise to take over the family business, and, with his wife and sister, to remain living in the family home. Werner, the son, bowing to paternal authority, is prepared to accept his father's proposals, although they are against his personal inclinations. But his wife, Johanna, demands a more thorough explanation as to why Von Gerlach is so intent on destroying their freedom, and by oath tying them to a way of life they would never have chosen for themselves. Up to this point the audience has been led to understand that Franz, the eldest son, is dead. Johanna's questions lead to the revelation that Franz, who returned home from the Russian front, decorated but defeated, has lived for the past thirteen years behind the bolted door of a single room. He admits no one except his sister, Leni, who takes him his meals of oysters and champagne, and with whom he has an incestuous relationship. He is living in a fantasy world of self-deception. *Les Séquestrés d'Altona* describes how he is finally forced to accept the truth about himself, and how this truth leads to his own and his father's suicides.

The play originally ran for over three hours, although Sartre shortened it in response to an almost unanimous appeal from the critics. It is an extremely difficult work to digest and understand at one sitting, for it deals with cancer, semi-madness, the nature of modern capitalism, family relationships, the generation gap, authority, power, free will, incest, love, torture. Though many of these themes are repeated in other works, *Les Séquestrés d'Altona* has two original features. It represents Sartre's first serious attempt to communicate the ideas and view of man outlined at the end of *Saint Genet: comédien et martyr* (see Chapter 8), and from the political point of view it is said to be his most successful attempt to put forward convincing left-wing arguments. Franz is like Jean Genet when he tries to explain his century to his imaginary tribunal of crabs. Sartre's intention, like Genet's, is to make the middle classes, who come to the theatre in search of amusement, suddenly aware of their own guilt, duplicity, and bad faith. Once one sees the play, it should come to life like a sleeping serpent with the warmth of arguments breathed into it.

The political parallel that can be drawn from the play is, as with *Les Troyennes*, France's involvement with Algeria. By dealing with the question of torture in a context apparently unconnected with France, Sartre manages to give general truth to his main thesis: whatever may be the apparent justification for torture, it can never be anything but an individual crime of common law. French officers sacrificing their military honour out of need for victory by organizing torture in Algeria may one day find themselves in Franz's absurd and tragic situation.

Another preoccupation of Sartre's which appears in *Les Séquestrés d'Altona* is the idea that the winner loses, and the loser wins. The father succeeds in seeing Franz only to discover that there can be no communication between them. Leni destroys the relationship between Johanna and Franz only to lose him altogether. These can be seen as other examples of Sartre's pessimistic view of human relationships.

The left-wing theme in *Les Séquestrés d'Altona* is the nature and corruption of modern capitalism. Sartre puts forward the idea that Franz is, above all else, the victim of the capitalist social system in which he lives. His father justifies his support for the Nazis by saying that they are the scum of the earth enthroned, but that they make war in order to find him markets. The other ironic outcome of capitalism is that the individual manipulator is ultimately made redundant by the managerial system. Von Gerlach knows he has ceased to be more than a cog in the wheel of a vast enterprise which has made him into a figurehead. He has trained his son to meet all the problems associated with building up a business, but, as soon as Franz is ready to take up his responsibilities in the business itself, he finds himself redundant.

Although one of the most enthusiastic reviews was written by Guy

Leclerc in *L'Humanité*, a Communist newspaper, praising Sartre for showing how the capitalist system is destroyed by its own contradictions, *Les Séquestrés d'Altona* is ultimately so pessimistic that one cannot suppose it expresses support for any party philosophy: when Franz comes to the end of his lies and self-defeat, he commits suicide. There is an insistence throughout on man's natural cruelty and sadism. Franz even confesses that, as he watched the Rabbi he was sheltering from the Nazis being killed, he found within his heart a kind of approval.

Sartre's plays have had a wide seminal influence, but while remaining a major figure in the French theatre, Sartre is ultimately not a great dramatist. None the less in using the theatre—as he uses the novel—as a vehicle for his ideas, he has produced a body of work that, although lacking some unifying emotional coherence, possesses weight, and is always passionate and inventive. The creation of character remains his main stumbling block; he cannot bring an independent and unique life to his personages, so they are not ultimately convincing. But his charting of the traps and ironies of human will, and his examination of pride, above all his analysis of decision, reveal perception of the highest order. Barrault has perceptively written that to Sartre he owes a deepening of his intellectual understanding of the way emotion works in the theatre:

> 'I had already come to think that everything serves a purpose, including play. Sartre brought a confirmation extending even to the emotions. Emotion is an extreme, a last resort, a limiting case of behaviour. If someone shows hostility to me, I puff out my chest, speak louder, put myself *into a temper*. I actually make myself stronger than I am. I am having recourse to a "magic" action . . . Briefly: the emotions are not states that come and add themselves at random to our behaviour, the emotions are actions.'

Three other 'committed' playwrights to be compared to Sartre, though unlike Sartre they are virtually unknown in England and America, are Aimé Césaire, Georges Michel, and Kateb Yacine.

AIMÉ CÉSAIRE, born in 1912 in the Antilles, was, like Arthur Adamov, first attached to the Surrealist movement, but later became more strongly involved with his own people's struggle for liberation from French colonial rule. Crowds in the Antilles have cheered him in the same breath as General de Gaulle, and he has written a famous biography of the black Jacobin Toussaint Louverture, which has been publicly mocked by André Malraux. He now lives in Paris where he is Martinique's deputy in the National Assembly; a one-time member of the French Communist party, he resigned in 1956 over Algeria, writing to Thorez that he wanted Marxism and Communism to serve the Black people, and not the other way about. He and the Haitian Communist poet Jacques Roumain are considered the finest black poets writing in the French language, and Césaire writes with an epic strength deriving its authority, as with Fanon who was his close friend and admirer, directly from the struggles of the tiny islands of the French West Indies for political autonomy. As an insurgent declares in one of Césaire's poems:

And the voice told us that through the ages Europe
has stuffed us with lies and swelled us with pestilence,
Yet it's not true man's work is over,
That we're parasites on life,
That we must get in step with everybody else
Man's best work is only just about to begin . . .

Unlike Sartre, he is an optimist, but he would agree with Marx
that social revolution should draw its inspiration from the future instead of the past.

Césaire's best known plays are *La Tragédie du roi Christophe*
(The Tragedy of King Christopher, 1963) a black protest play, and
Une Saison au Congo (A Season in the Congo, 1966) an outstanding
work celebrating the life, and mourning the death, of Patrice Lumumba. It achieves a balance which is all too rare between left-wing
idealism, and the depiction of colonial villainy. The reason for this is
that the form Césaire has chosen is near to the medieval morality
play. Lumumba is a mixture of Christ and Everyman, the Belgians
are the stock buffoon agents of Satanic power (Satan himself is Uncle
Sam). Battle is waged between innocence and evil, knowledge, truth,
and expediency, until the martyrdom of Lumumba is sealed. It
manages to avoid the pitfalls of the documentary play, too heavy an
insistence on facts with a corresponding lifelessness of character and,
even more impressively, it avoids the platform aspect which converts
the playwright's material to propagandist ends.

From the first moment we see Lumumba being savagely beaten by
a pair of Belgian guards, we know whose side Césaire wants us to be
on. But he never harangues us. He leaves his characters alone to get
on with it, and human qualities emerge instead of doctrinal points.
Compassion for the struggling ignorance of the Third World is all the
more effective and thought-provoking to watch, because it is instinctive and not in any way clouded with remedies.

Césaire's poetic gifts come to the fore in his underlining of his
hero's individual qualities, for Lumumba's greatest gift is his deep
imaginative grasp of the soul of his people. He wants the Congo to be
Congolese, lackey of neither East nor West, freed from the
suffocating machinations of international finance, freed from its own
sense of inferiority. Lumumba tries to bring self-esteem to his
people, wrench out of them a sense of dignity. The betrayal of
Congolese independence by the great powers, the terrible decline
from the exhilaration of a new liberty to sordid massacres, and the
furious spoil of civil war, have a decisive and controlled inevitability.

But the greatest pleasure and strength of *Une Saison au Congo*
remains in the writing, which ranges from simple direct satire in the
political scenes, through the most extraordinary flights of brilliant
rhetoric, to witty and poetic evocations of the Congo. It conjures up
jungle and shanty-town, the majestic river itself:

Père Congo,
tu charries des fleurs, des îles.
Qu'est-ce qui gonfle ton cœur gris
et de hoquets te brise? . . .

As well as tawdry nationalism, there is cynical political manoeuvring, and splendid passionate confrontations between black Congolese, Belgians, and Dag Hammarskjöld.

GEORGES MICHEL, born in 1926, was Sartre's discovery, and of several important plays, *Aggression* (1966), which has been performed at the TNP, is both typical and powerful. It deals with the frustrations of teenage gangs, and the frustration is shown to be interchangeable with the freedom, and directly proportional to it. Naturally enough, it is a subject dear to Sartre's heart and he contributed a glowing programme note for the production in 1967.

The act of violence is *Aggression's* touch of brilliance; it is society itself which commits it. There comes a moment when all the pop culture elements—two screens with marriage and sex adverts flashed simultaneously on them, wild popping lights of a funfare and, most importantly, four lurid shop windows—advance on the cowed gang of young people. With deranged 'admen' voices they provoke the kids into breaking the windows; the image is a lasting one, for it shows the present violating the soul of youth. Michel supplies his director and cast with plenty of scope for the manipulation of stage effects; film, music, industrial noise in a factory scene where one of the gang is assimilated into the brown-coated world of conformism (represented by a chorus of timid and guilt-ridden elders), as well as political agit-prop (cars pushed across stage, statesmen screaming from daises), make it a well-sustained and lively piece.

It comes to rest in one last gentle scene where park grass is unrolled on the stage and we see the gang pushing their prams through an obstacle race of prohibitive signs: 'pélouse interdite', 'défense de courir', 'défense de jouer au ballon', finally the bleak anonymous sign which somehow sums it all up, 'espace vert'. The time of youth is over.

The third writer, KATEB YACINE, born in Algeria in 1929, like Aimé Césaire identifies with the Third World, and he has written several plays and a novel which have at their centre a heroine called Nedjuma, who personifies (as Irish writers at the Abbey Theatre employed the colourful 'Cathleen ni Houlihan') a mythical Algeria. In *Les Ançêtres redoublent de férocité* (The Ancestors Redouble their Ferocity, 1967) the Algerian War itself is explored with flamboyant ritualism. Like Césaire, Yacine writes in rich poetic imagery and employs chanting choruses, as well as back-projections of photographs. Around a skeleton of a horse unfolds a tribal re-enactment of the 'mana' of war, a chilling charade of death played out with biting indigenous vitality. But one senses too great a degree of derivation behind the writing, not only in shades of Genet's *Les Paravents*, but also Brecht's *Mother Courage*.

4 Theatre of choice (2)

Marie: Why do you go on punishing me?
Georges: I punish you because you are suffering.

From *Demain il fera jour*

In the post-war English theatre, John Whiting is the nearest or most comparable writer to HENRI DE MONTHERLANT, though on a far less heroic and successful scale. Whiting died first, at a much earlier age. Both were aloof from their contemporaries, both were concerned with proud and egoistic heroes, and both wrote in a heightened, though not in any way flamboyant, style. Whiting died tragically of cancer in his early forties after starting to write in an entirely new manner influenced by the cinema which he hoped desperately would bring him nearer to a mass audience. He was a traditionalist in an age which despised tradition, which preferred the ephemeral menace of a Pinter, or the extended purple tirades of an Osborne.

Montherlant was a born winner, and was luckier in so far as he was French. Born in 1896, he died in the autumn of 1972 by shooting himself through the mouth after losing the sight of his left eye in a car accident; his doctor had told him that if he tired his good eye, by reading and writing, he would ruin it and become blind; ceasing to desire sexually, and ceasing to write was 'death in life.' But unlike Whiting, he had lived to the age of seventy-six and produced a monumental body of work that is sure to last; he is a legend, both for the active part he took in life as an athlete, a soldier, and a bullfighter, and for his contemplative achievements as one of the foremost stylists, in the novel and the theatre, of his day.

It is probably idle speculation to ask why so eminent and self-controlled a figure as this aristocrat of Catalan blood should have taken his own life. His religious beliefs were contradictory, and constantly changing. He said he was both a Christian and a hedonist, but in the final reckoning, sensuality, and its accompanying coldness and distance from other people, would appear to have dominated. He liked every thing that 'excited the mind' and 'quickened the blood', and in such a way he thought the attempt to 'reconcile Pan and Jesus Christ will always be a sovereign exercise for the non-believer'. In an early short story, *The Death of Peregrinos*, he writes of a man whose life has been a signal failure, and who therefore is determined to make a success of his death. Montherlant's own sometimes disagreeable sense of superiority, not only brought down on him the wrath of Simone de Beauvoir, who failed to notice the double-edge of his irony towards women, but made him feel an outcast to many aspects of society; in the same story he quotes both Goethe ('Polite society, which is loath to tolerate any eminent man in its vicinity') and

Tolstoy ('Sextus the Fifth's crutch must be the pilgrim's staff of every outstanding man') as exceptional and misunderstood figures in their own time.

Exceptional and misunderstood Montherlant also was, but he seemed by no means unhappy about it; one suspects he might even have encouraged it, for there clung about him none of the sensitivity of the romantic artist, and criticism did not appear to wound him. Byron wickedly claimed in *Don Juan* that Keats was 'snuffed out' by an adverse article, but when the café-singer, Bonnard, sang in his New Year wishes for 1926 'let's hope that swine Montherlant doesn't publish another damn book, and if by bad luck he does, it's posthumous!' Montherlant himself did not turn a hair. Only bulls could hurt him, it seemed, for at that very same moment he lay in bed critically gored through the lung. One of his first plays to be staged, by Jean Vilar, was a treatment of the mythological story of a woman who was sexually enraptured with a bull (*Pasiphaë*, 1936, revived in 1974). The main character of one of his novels, *Les Bestiaires*, loves a bull more than he does the heroine.

Montherlant's egoism, the degree to which his own self was the very centre of his universe, had an amplitude and design which conjures up images of the Renaissance, like Cellini or the Medici family. He wished to be effective in every direction; 'a healthy soul' he wrote in a summary of his philosophy to which characteristically he gave the title, *Hold Fast to all things while keeping each in its proper place*, 'with that basic simplicity which both distinguishes and makes possible great things, will always be flexible, copious and vigorous enough to reconcile, in a higher and joyous unity, most of the so-called contradictions which give pause to many of the spineless creatures we see around us.' He was often accused by his enemies of being right wing, and even, during the Second World War, of being a collaborator. But this was not true. His mien and manner did suggest unbending will, though the critic of the *Sunday Times*, Harold Hobson who called on him at his home in the Quai Voltaire in 1960, has testified to his friendly and modest manner. He adopted, or expressed, many attitudes violently contradictory to the traditional attitudes of his class. He despised the middle class because dishonesty was a way of life with them; he hated capitalism (after 1926) saying that the spontaneous generation of money had a nasty smell about it. In 1929 he produced a novel with a working-class background, called *Moustique, ou L'Hôpital* to show how poor people die when they cannot afford to buy their own medicine. When he won a valuable literary prize he gave it away to French Colonial troops and the Moroccan rebels they had just crushed: both sides had performed their duty and fought for their principles, he noted. It gave him great pleasure, he wrote later, when he found out what few Christians would find reprehensible today, that in the Christian Middle Ages money-lending was forbidden, and even now, in Muslim canon law, it is still forbidden. He wrote a masterly short story exposing cruel anti-semitic attitudes in the First World War.

'A play' he wrote 'only interests if its external action, reduced to the greatest simplicity, is an excuse for the exploration of man; but not if the playwright has given himself the job of imagining and mechanically constructing a plot—only if his concern is to show, with the maximum of truth, intensity, and depth, a certain number of movements of the human soul.'

This directive is most faithfully followed in *Demain il fera jour* (Tomorrow the Dawn) which was first published in 1949, though performed earlier. An extraordinarily spare and athletic work, it is conceived and written with a direct and clear sense of line. One suspects that, were it to be translated and performed in English, it would sound too abstract, lacking the dramatic 'roughage' English audiences appear to need.

The main character, Georges, is a lawyer, and he equivocates in his feelings towards his bastard son, Gillou, who wants to join the Resistance. The play takes place in Paris, in the summer of 1944, when the Allies have already landed in Normandy and are advancing on Paris, so there is straight away a kind of ambivalence in attitude (often voiced in England but rarely in France) towards the Resistance. Gillou is told that, if he really had wanted to be a hero, he should have joined earlier; and yet Georges, who is himself suspected of being a collaborator with the Germans, or with the Pétainists, knows that, if Gillou does join the patriots, it will clear him of punishment.

Montherlant, we know, was accused of favouring the Fascists; he was a friend of the Italian aristocrat poet and theorist d'Annunzio. In the postscript to this play he sets out the various forms of bad odour he expected to arouse. Georges is, in fact, an extremely unsympathetic character and, because of this, Montherlant thought he would incur the fury of all ex-collaborators; communists would be amused at his turncoat approach, while the solid middle class would be shocked at his lovingly drawn portrait of a young communist.

This was typical of Montherlant, who really liked to outrage everyone, and, finally, assert his own independence of all political allegiances. He liked to think of the public as the bull, whom he challenged to gore him. But besides the twisting and flipping of his multi-coloured cape, which he indulged in with steely precision in one preface and postscript after another (a playwright such as Arnold Wesker, who has turned on his critics, should examine these, for they provide superb models of condescending intelligence), *Demain il fera jour* is a gripping work, remorselessly concentrated, and very readable. It suffers from too much discussion without physical or concrete examples, or a subtext of minute actions such as one finds in David Mercer, for example the cooking of meals in *Let's Murder Vivaldi*, or an imagery that brings another dimension to the thoughts and inner psychology.

But the constantly changing inflections of motive in Georges are fascinating; his moods, his egotism towards his son, his refusal to see him as a person in his own right, which makes the boy weak and obedient to his will, as well as his barely concealed distaste for his suffering mistress, who clings to the boy, are all vividly alive.

Intricacies of motive are strong in those works which have a modern setting. The degree to which Montherlant was obsessed by the idea of sacrifice is overwhelmingly evident in *La Reine morte* (Queen in Death, 1942). Ferrante, King of Portugal, takes very great care in exploring the soul and character of the lovely young Inès de Castro, who has secretly married his son and heir, Pedro. Dramatic interest is cunningly sustained until the very last encounter of Ferrante and his daughter-in-law, before Ferrante arranges to have her murdered: but here the story begins to sag terribly.

Typically, Montherlant becomes too concerned with Ferrante's private morbidities of power: this turns the hero into a self-indulgent monster, as he loses grip on his circumstances without any strong pressure from outside. Again, Montherlant cannot resist the temptation to wring the very last ounce of selfishness from his people. True, there are one or two set-backs in the plot, like the surprise invasion of some Africans at Tavira, but the central dilemma Montherlant constructs is not logically and ruthlessly pursued.

The dilemma itself comes from the position Pedro the son and Inès are placed in by their clandestine marriage, and by Ferrante's implacable will to make Pedro marry the headstrong young Infanta of Navarre, whose preliminary refusal by Pedro evokes the splendid rhetoric of pride which Montherlant is so marvellous at deploying. 'Did you know', she says, 'that in Navarre, we die from humiliation?'

This situation is kept simmering with some degree of fascinating complexity with scenes in which Pedro and Inès are allowed to meet, with Ferrante refusing to kill Inès outright, with the hidden explosive secret which Ferrante does not yet know, namely that she is pregnant. There is also a sensual and impulsively rich lesbian scene when the Infanta tries to seduce Inès and to persuade her to return to her beloved Navarre. Inès, in her innocence, refuses. Her sense of truth, her love, her foolish and finally betrayed trust in the goodness of Ferrante, make her stand her ground.

In *La Reine morte*, the father–son involvement which makes *Demain il fera jour* and its predecessor *Fils de personne* (No Man's Son, 1943) such compelling psychological documents, is not pursued between Ferrante and Pedro. Montherlant fills in the historically stretched canvas with courtiers and page-boys, and they are not very productive of exciting incidental action—Montherlant had not really much power in wielding events on the grand scale. But the portrait of Inès, her sense of openness, in contrast to the hypocrisies and bad faith at court, her joy in her unborn child, are very moving. When this play was first performed, at the Comédie-Française in 1942, Inès was played by Madeleine Renaud.

The problems of translating and staging Montherlant in English are considerable. *La Guerre civile* (Civil War, 1965), about the conflict between Pompey and Caesar, shows Montherlant's methods both at their strongest and weakest. It is exciting in its paradoxical comments on the nature of public affairs, especially those spoken by Cato, who considers the arguments on both sides to be lacking in justification. But it is weak in the drawing of the characters. Few of the characters lose Montherlant's highly egoistical and personal flavour. The image becomes one not so much of pre-Christian Rome, as of the playwright reflecting on the divided opinions of a nation locked in civil strife. This is something with which France, since the Revolution, is only too familiar. But no central issue comes to dominate the play, as it does in *La Reine morte*. As a result, except for the death of Acilius, the outcome is not gripping.

In *La Ville dont le prince est un enfant* (1951) Montherlant's 'haute bourgeoise' psychology is most successfully married to the lofty classicism which makes him a direct inheritor of the Racine and Corneille tradition (Gabriel Marcel called Georges in *Fils de personne* a 'Cornelian father'). *La Ville* was the third play in what the author has described as his Catholic trilogy, the other being *Le Maître de Santiago* (The Master of Santiago, 1948), which was successfully played in English, with Sir Donald Wolfit vibrating his larynx in tune with the spiritual aspirations of the vicar general, and *Port-Royal*, which the Comédie-Française have successfully revived in 1974. Published first in book form, like many of Montherlant's works, it had prodigious sales (over 125,000 copies) before it finally came to be played at the Théâtre Michel, where it ran for several seasons, and then later in the World Theatre Season at the Aldwych. The town of the title refers to a Catholic boys' college outside Paris, and, in stringent form, are examined the motives which lead an Abbé to break up a relationship between an elder boy and a younger, and his contamination of that relationship with his own selfish emotions. To some degree, it is a repetition of the basic triangle of *La Reine morte*, and was, Montherlant claimed, based on an experience which happened to him at school forty years before.

Finally, when the drama has been pushed to its limits, and the elder boy expelled, the Abbé is carpeted by his superior—in a majestic scene of torn-apart motivation, or altruism exposed as egoism. The pessimism is deeper than Graham Greene's, whose priest heroes ultimately have some saving grace which awakens compassion. The logic of probing the truth in a man's soul is less entertaining and more forceful than in Greene: beneath the overwhelming and slightly sickly sense of guilt that hangs over it, *La Ville*'s strength is in its simplicity.

The control of loyalties in Montherlant's world of man and God (women definitely do not enter into it) has a repressed sexuality which itself generates considerable tension. The writing mounts carefully to its emotional climaxes, which explode with generous and powerful fury. Though the form satisfies, the feeling while watching the play is close to that of being shut up in a box of bad odours: at any moment, one feels, the drama might flower into abhorrent attitudes, so craftily is it loaded with evil, and balanced against the impartiality of the church. Yet the balance *is* held and *La Ville* remains Montherlant's really outstanding achievement in the theatre.

5 The cynics (I)

> 'The impossibility of reply is itself the reply, it's your very being
> which is bursting out, spreading. Plunge into astonishment and
> stupefaction without end; this way you can be endless.'
>
> *Le Roi se meurt*

The problem of the French playwrights of the so-called 'absurd' is in-
tegration. They are, without exception, exiles from their home country in a foreign land: immigrants, or the children of immigrants.
Adamov from Russia, Ionesco from Romania, Beckett from Ireland
(the same is true of two of the foremost playwrights of the absurd in
England, Harold Pinter and Tom Stoppard). The emotion that informs all their work is the emotion of the displaced person: the logic
that is common to all of them is the logic of the uprooted. This may
account for their extraordinary hold over the American academic
mind.

In the plays of ARTHUR ADAMOV (1908–70) man becomes victim
of his own nightmares in an unreal world which increases his terror.
In *La Grande et la petite manœuvre* (1950) the main character who is
obedient to mysterious words of command voluntarily undergoes
mutilation. *Le Professeur Taranne* contains no characters with individuality. First performed at Lyons in 1953 where it was directed
by Roger Planchon, it is about a teacher who is accused wrongfully of
sexually exhibiting himself; he ends up committing the offence of
which he is accused. Adamov has written that *Le Professeur Taranne*
is the transposition of a dream he once had, and it is hardly more than
this—violent abstract, essentially surreal in effect. There is also a
kind of mechanical unreality about *Le Ping-Pong*, performed in 1955
at the Théâtre des Noctambules, Paris. Adamov introduces political
allegory into an essentially facetious tale of two young men, Victor
and Arthur, who love playing pinball and try to rig a pinball consortium. The lives of the two of them, as well as three others, come to
depend entirely on this machine. They pass through various ups and
downs—the machine breaks down, they try to improve it, they have
to take other jobs—then part of the consortium dies, or leaves. Finally, Victor and Arthur are left alone, aged seventy, playing ping-pong;
they dispense with the net and the rackets; they even come to forget
the table; during the last wild, free-for-all game Victor has a heart
attack.

Sartre, who disliked Adamov's early work, discerned a change for
the better in *Le Ping-Pong*; in it, he said, Adamov was starting to do
something positive. He felt him beginning to sympathize with his
characters: this is certainly true of Arthur, the sensitive young man
who is corrupted from the finer possibilities of his nature by the
machinations of the consortium.

In Adamov's later plays the Brechtian influence completely over-takes the Artaud influence. *Johnnie Brown* reminds one strongly of *The Rise and Fall of the State of Mahagonny*: it is an attack on a system. The eponymous hero is accused of murdering a black man, called Tom Guinness. Johnnie Brown, Tom Guinness, Jimmie Madison ... the names of the characters have an unreal, satirical ring. Then, typically, a quarter of the way through, Adamov goes off at a tangent: again into the private psychosis, the strange Freudian pattern of his earlier plays. The main problem is that Adamov is un-funny. His didacticism lacks lightness of touch. A more serious criticism is that his Marxism seems to have been adopted as a theoretical escape from the dead-end nature of absurdist writing, but his talent could not match his theory.

Adamov worshipped Brecht's *The Exception and the Rule*: 'The spectacle of this clash—of employer and worker—of the gross dis-crepancy between the small deceitful reasoning and the real poverty of men; and the spectacle of the link, both logical and laughable, between the cause and the effect, has never been better presented on the stage.' He failed to see the central flaw in this play, namely that it does not succeed in convincing in the theatre itself: it is patently a demonstration rather than an enactment or imitation of an action. It makes men into insects. Adamov may well fancifully elaborate his in-tentions with *Le Ping-Pong* ... 'I could, for example, have used the subject ... to unmask, through the pin-table consortium, the society that produced it; or rather I could not have done that, for it was not until I was writing the play that I began to glimpse the possibility of a theatre which would expose the duplicity which in this case in-volved persuading people that a given object resulted from a genuine need, whereas in fact it created a false demand for itself' (*Ici et maintenant*, Paris, 1964. But in practice, in the work itself, clarity and effectiveness are marred by a zealous desire to include too many precise examples, too much detail. There is something frantic about Adamov's development: instead of simplifying and gaining in strength and ease, his vision has become cluttered, more tortured, and more confused.

Adamov died in 1970, the year Ionesco was honoured by being made a member of the French Academy. EUGENÈ IONESCO (born 1912) is above all the playwright of personal obsessions. Sartre has pointed out that to call him, and the other writers associated with him, writers of the absurd is itself absurd, as 'none of them consider human life and the world as an absurdity' (*Mythe et réalité du théâtre*, 1966). Only Camus can truly be considered a writer of the absurd; his whole philosophy of life revolves round a notion of absur-dity. But the theatre of the absurd is a useful label, as Martin Esslin has demonstrated in his influential book. How Ionesco differs from Artaud and from other surrealists is that he restores the word to its prime role of appealing to the imagination. Ionesco takes it a stage further than Claudel or Audiberti. His theatre is primarily a show-piece of the unconscious, to show how the unconscious is structured like a wild and wilful language which takes over everything. He demonstrates the truth of what Heidegger wrote: 'Man behaves as if he was the creator and master of language, while it is language, on the contrary, which is, and which rests his sovereign' (quoted in Sartre's *Un Théâtre de situations*, 1973). In Ionesco's plays it is not character that develops, but language, as the dialogue spreads its tentacles across the cardboard human shapes, tying them up, crushing them under its tyranny. It makes characters do what they have no intention of doing. In *La Leçon* (The Lesson, 1951) the teacher murders his pupil at the end of the lesson, which is something he never started out meaning to do: it is language which has driven him on inexorably to do this. Ionesco shows us the internal contradictions in man's nature when put up against the nature of language: 'language is the hero: it is the main character. It is king in exact proportion to the extent that theatre has dethroned man.'

Dramatic works may well be seminal even though they have only been seen by a few thousand people. This was true of *La Cantatrice chauve* (The Bald Primadonna, 1950) and *La Leçon* in their early days: both have now been running at the Théâtre de la Huchette for eighteen years. In a programme note to Romain Weingarten's *L'Eté*, Ionesco denounced documentary theatre (the 'dernier cri' of realism, he called it), and what he termed the 'coarse' productions of Peter Brook; nevertheless it is his own form of theatre which seems to be on the wane in the middle seventies, rather than the theatre of his rivals, the realists. It is fascinating to note that in France, as in England—though far less consciously in England—playwriting incorporates a whole philosophy of life. 'Reality is not realistic: realism is a style,' Ionesco writes, but he is right only as far as he goes. Realism, and naturalism, are ways of life: style is the man himself.

The 'king of the surrealist conjurers', Tynan has called Ionesco. *Rhinocéros*, his first full-length play, presented by Barrault at the Odéon-Théâtre de France in 1959, should have been his crowning triumph, but it was the beginning of his abdication. It is entirely an expressionistic play: Bérenger, the central character, becomes a rhinoceros. Why he does so, we never really know: did Ionesco mean him to suggest that Bérenger was becoming a fascist or a communist, conforming to all other rhinoceroses that were around him? Is the rhinoceros language? Why does Bérenger resist, does he signify the individual in the face of the impersonal destructive forces that threaten man? As Esslin reports in *The Theatre of the Absurd*, *Rhinocéros* may well represent Ionesco's feelings about Romania before he left in 1938:

> 'As usual, I went back to personal obsessions, I remembered that in the course of my life I have been very much struck by what one might call the current of opinion, by its rapid evolution, its power of contagion, which is that of a real epidemic. People allow themselves suddenly to be invaded by a new religion, a doctrine, a fanaticism ... At such moments we witness a veritable mental mutation ... history has shown us during the last quarter of a century that people thus transformed not only resemble rhinos, but really become rhinoceroses.'

Esslin himself goes further in finding that the play mocks the individualist who considers himself superior. This is where the play 'transcends the over-simplification of propaganda and becomes a valid statement of the fatal entanglement, the basic inescapability and absurdity of the human condition.' But an intellectual recognition is not necessarily an experience of the heart: 'valid statements' do not necessarily make for moving theatre: never when watching Ionesco have I experienced any sense of the absurdity of the human condition. None of the characters in Ionesco's plays have, in the theatre itself, struck me as ever being human. Their language is human: they themselves are puppets driven by impersonal fear or despair. Human characteristics can only be grafted on to the characters Ionesco creates by a painful and skilful operation. Often, in spite of the efforts of the performers, they do not stick.

Ionesco's work offers, like that of the other playwrights of the absurd, with their ambiguities, and their tantalizing and sometimes infuriating incompleteness, an excellent hunting-ground for critical exegesis and evaluation (Adamov is the best example of someone who has been more written about than performed). One has yet to be convinced that Ionesco has written, or will ever write, a satisfactory full-length play. The drift of his idea can usually be grasped in the first twenty or thirty minutes, the rest is often repetitive, though some of the subsequent effects are chilling or amusing, or sometimes visually shattering. But in spite of the artful elaboration, the spectators' emotions are suspended, or alienated, in a far more hostile way than in Brecht. Even the terror itself is de-humanized, though when it is not, as in *Tueur sans gages* (The Killer, 1959), Ionesco is seen at his very best.

In Ionesco's later work there is a distinct falling off. In *Jeux de massacre* (Carnival Slaughter) produced at the Montparnasse Gaston-Baty Théâtre in 1970, the thin charade of death repeats itself endlessly: it is a play about death and, in spite of being acclaimed by every Paris critic, it does not sustain its length. The opening is brilliant: we were shown, in Jorge Lavelli's production on a multi-level set, a modern high-rise block transformed into a vast bank of rabbit-hutches. It was early morning. Everyone threw his hutch open, and the day breathed in. Couples took to the street, gossiping away. Gradually, in snatches, a subject emerged: the plague started first to encroach on everyone conversationally. Then a baby was discovered dead. People accused one another of murder. They began to kill, or to drop dead of real or imagined plague. Death, a morality figure in black, arrived on a bicycle. By the end of the scene the stage was littered with corpses.

This scene makes—and did make—a perfect statement. However, in the dozen or more scenes that follow, there is no dramatic progression from the first. There are orators, gaolers, nurses, lovers, old people, politicians, the survivors (at the very end) who all, in various stages of hysteria, finally drop dead. Even Death, in grotesque and parodic fulfilment of the words of the John Donne sonnet, finally dies. In a grand finale the cast, each of whom must have been called upon already to die in at least several different disguises, succumbs collectively to this extreme demonstration of holocausts.

Speculating on Ionesco's meaning in *Jeux de massacre* would be flattering, one suspects, an underlying self-indulgence. On the stage, it lacks the challenging reticence of his early short masterpieces like *La Cantatrice chauve* and *La Leçon*. Without any social or human content, Ionesco's theatre seems to have become merely an exercise in style: death itself is never more than phantasmagoric. None of the characters arouses any sympathy: they all run away like rats in flight from microbes. The intellectual study of fear that remains (Victor Hugo said drama should make 'thought the bread of the people'; Ionesco has made it the bicarbonate of intellectuals) is extraordinarily narrow-minded. The play appears to be saying that, confronted with fear, we all become fascists. This impression is deepened by a film script written and performed by Ionesco (shown in 1974), and called *La Vase* (The Vase). An elderly writer is pursued, besieged by his terrors, in a country retreat: the mail, delivered daily by the postman, piles up against the front door like a snow-drift. There seem to be two Ionescos visible in the film, with strongly differing appearances. The first is a middle-aged, reasonably vigorous chap who wears a discreet toupée and marches down country lanes inhaling the air, exchanging cheerful greetings with the villagers. The other is a bald, decaying creature harassed by fantasy and despair who can do nothing but feel his pulse and who eats old bread dipped in even older shaving water. This tour of Ionesco's haunted house, his own private House of Usher, and his final rock-climbing escapade—and his very grand and decorous suicide, where he simply slides under stagnant, weed-filled water—demonstrate that he has passed over absurdity in favour of disgust. Although at the end of the film there is a token of resistance, as there was in *Rhinocéros*, when his still breathing nostrils poke out from otherwise amorphous mud and he exclaims 'Je recommencerai', it is self-pity and self-torture which dominate.

Ionesco swivels his ravaged head round in front of the camera as if he were toasting a current bun in front of a fire: no angle, he seems to be saying, must be spared the view. He probes the bags under his eyes, he takes off his shirt to show the sagging flesh: cigarette stubs accumulate on the beds of his house, weeds force their way through the neatly tiled floor, livers rot, arms decompose. Of course he might deliberately have been making a fool of himself, but there is nothing funny about it. The outward trappings of his earlier works were at least humorous and delightful. But these now seem to have been stripped away, very much as in Tardieu's surrealist play *La Serrure* (The Keyhole, 1955) the stripper whom a voyeur watches through a keyhole goes beyond her clothes, to strip herself of all her flesh and her organs. A stone's throw away from where, in the winter of 1974, I saw *La Vase, La Cantatrice chauve* and *La Leçon* were playing for the 5,600th time. The eighteen years' run of these two plays and the first projection of *La Vase* had spanned the rise of the theatre of the absurd, its flowering—appropriately and absurdly enough, perhaps never quite a full flowering—and the beginning of its decline.

6 The cynics (2)

'I shall die of a burst of voices
splitting my ears open.
I shall die of muffled wounds
Inflicted at 2 a.m.
By bald and indecisive killers.'

Boris Vian

ROMAIN WEINGARTEN was born in 1926 of a Polish father and a Breton mother. His play *L'Eté* (Summer, 1965) is generally considered to be one of the best new French plays of recent years; unlike Ionesco who declared Weingarten's *Akara*, which was first performed as far back as 1948, one of the pioneer and early important works of the 'nouveau théâtre', Weingarten is preoccupied with human happiness. Ionesco denies his characters identity; he disrupts atmosphere; he plays the buffoon with every kind of continuity. Weingarten puts the same means to a much more personal exploration, in *L'Eté*, of two children on the threshold of adolescence. A charming house-exterior and a garden, with gold cut-out lights intermingling with leaf green, is the setting for their observation of the two lovers who arrive to stay at the house. The lovers, who are constantly spied upon for six days and nights, never appear. A pair of talking cats, which fulfil the function of *agents provocateurs* as well as that of witty commentators, are Weingarten's most ingenious invention. The lovers arrive, go to bed together, lose a ring, quarrel, part, and leave the house. Invisible to us, their actions reverberate strongly in the children's tentative and painful gropings towards a relationship, their growing awareness of love and death. The boy is somewhat of a simpleton, able to talk with the cats; the girl dreams of love. The interplay between the reality of their states and the watching cats, sleek-coated, spiteful and affectionately mannered, shows how Weingarten has joined the tradition of absurdity on to a real situation.

Compared with the simple and elegant wit of *L'Eté*, *Akara* is a much harsher work: in it the cat is the victim of persecution, a symbol rather than the delightful anthropomorphized reality. The text capers along with complexity: 'Nous passons en quatre, double la somme en sept pince oreilles, recapitulons en huit: Floche marnière, quinte minette, fodre-fil, Migre mort, je gagne, c'est moi qui gagne', is a particularly extravagant and untranslatable example, and today it seems out-dated. But his latest plays, *Alice* and *Dans les jardins du Luxembourg* (1970) continue the delicate poetic tradition of *L'Eté*. Weingarten is very much a conservationist of the theatre's magic. His plays appeal to the imagination of the actor: no two finer performances were to be seen in Paris in the 1967–68 season than those of Nicolas Bataille and Weingarten himself as the cats at the Théâtre de Poche; *L'Eté* was so successful it was revived for two successive seasons.

BORIS VIAN (1920–59) with his cynicism and subdued ferocity, typified an era of disillusionment for the young; although he died in 1959, aged only 39, his work has had a considerable influence since his death. An early novel, *L'Ecume des jours*, written in 1947, has sold 465,000 copies since 1964. To a large extent during his life Vian was more a phenomenon than a writer: his life-style was far from that of an innocent and spoiled romantic, like Dylan Thomas, who also died before he reached forty. He was Parisian to the core—sophisticated, contemptuous—and he swooped down on all the various genres, poetry, drama, song-writing, the short story, the novel, and snapped them up with a kind of Olympian disdain. He was also a jazz trumpeter of considerable prowess, whose attachment to the post-war St Germain set made him into a superman of culture to rank alongside such figures as Cocteau, Artaud, Piaf.

In Jacques Baratier's famous film, *Désordre a vingt ans*, Vian's character is illuminated in several extraordinary sequences—an interview, in English, on the snow-clad terrace of his house behind the Moulin Rouge; singing, in that strangely flat rasping tone, the great pacifist song of all time, *Le Déserteur*, which he composed himself; playing till dawn at Le Tabou because he could not bear to go home and face the fact that he was nearing death from a serious heart condition. He attacked everything and everybody, his disdain turning, scorpion-like, in the end on himself and his own works, of which he said 'C'est rien tout ça ... Rien quoi. Vraiment rien.'

His first three books, which he wrote under the pen-name of Vernon Sullivan and which he claimed were 'translated from the American', showed him out-gunning Raymond Chandler and Mickey Spillane at their own game. *J'irai cracher sur vos tombes* was banned for immorality in 1949; *L'Ecume des jours* is now a book seriously studied in schools, though the extreme Left rejects it as being too bourgeois. His best play, *Les Bâtisseurs d'empire* (The Empire Builders), was only performed for the first time after his death in 1959 at the Théâtre Récamier, and later in London by the Royal Shakespeare Company. The idea comes from the familiar American horror movie in which a group of people, in this case a family, are threatened by a mystery noise, which will not leave them alone, and claims them, one after another, as its victim. With them throughout is a pathetic creature called the Schmürz. They ignore the Schmürz except for beating him savagely time and again.

More burlesque are *L'Equarrissage pour tous* (Knackering for Everyone, 1944) and *Le Goûter des généraux* (The Generals' Tea-party, 1965) in which generals make up a war for their own amusement, and end by committing suicide in a game of Russian roulette. *Tête de Méduse* (Medusa's Head, 1951) centres on the old half-truth that masterpieces are reared on jealousy. The writer-hero sends his wife off deliberately to gore his sensibilities with her infidelities: schematic rather than fully realized, this contains some excellent dialogue which moves along, as much of Vian's work, at a breathless and unremitting pace. *Série blème* (Pale Range, 1952) injects slang into that holy untouchable of the academicians, the alexandrine: another writer-hero—James Monroe, the imaginary brother of Marilyn—protects his hard-won peace in a mountain chalet by bumping off a considerable number of would-be destroyers of solitude: toothpaste salesmen. In his last also posthumously published play *Le Chasseur français* (French Hunter, 1955) which is a detective musical comedy for philosophy students and a horse (which is listed in the list of *dramatis personae* as a philosophy graduate), there are still the word-games which derive from Alfred Jarry, still the *macabrerie*, the acid lyrics, and the soap-opera absurdities. But Vian's most gripping work remains *Les Bâtisseurs d'empire* with its vision of the narrowing world, as the pursuing noise drives the family into nothingness. Finally the father is left alone, until, in the terrifying last moments, he himself is obliterated. 'The noise,' writes Vian in the final stage direction 'invades the scene, and with it, darkness. And perhaps the door also opens and there enter, in the darkness, vague silhouettes of other schmürzes'. . . .

JEAN TARDIEU is far too little performed: but he is by far the most innovatory and technically versatile of the playwrights of the absurd. As Esslin in his excellent study of Tardieu points out, two of the earliest plays, *Qui est là?* (Who's There, 1947) and *La Politesse inutile* (Useless Politeness, 1947), present to some extent the same situations as Ionesco's *La Cantatrice chauve* and *La Leçon*. If we look at the texts themselves, the similarities are even more striking. The first speech of the father in *Qui est là?* runs as follows:

LE PÈRE: Je suis le père. Voici ma femme et voici mon fils. Au dehors la nuit est froide et longue, c'est l'hiver, mais ici nous nous rechauffons les uns les autres, et nous sommes assis à cette table pour apaiser notre faim, en échangeant des propos affectueux.

Un silence.

LE PÈRE: (*Il fait à lui seul la demande et al réponse, tandis que la mère et le fils se taisent, l'œil fixe*). Qu'as-tu fait ce matin? J'ai été à l'école. Et toi? Je suis allée au marché. Qu'as-tu trouvé? Des légumes plus cher qu'hier et de la viande à meilleur compte. . . .

In *La Cantatrice chauve*, it is Madame Smith who talks first but she adopts the same abrupt, informative posture:

MME SMITH: Tiens, il est neuf heures. Nous avons mangé de la soupe, du poisson, des pommes de terre au lard, de la salade anglaise. Les enfants ont bu de l'eau anglaise. Nous avons bien mangé, ce soir. . . .

It is as if Ionesco's garrulity is filling out Tardieu's pure idea with humour and flesh. Too often the brilliant notions of the older writer (Tardieu was born in 1903, Ionesco 1912) fail to take off and excite the imagination in the way Ionesco can. For instance, *La Serrure* (The Keyhole, 1955) is an extraordinarily potent image of contemporary voyeurist tendencies, but there remains something wooden and ornate in the dialogue. A client comes to a very specialized form of brothel and watches through an enormous keyhole a beautiful woman taking off her clothes. His expectation is whetted by the madame, and when she has gone he is able to begin his curious vigil. He has by now become fearfully excited.

'It's really her. Her! Just as I've always seen her, just as she has appeared a thousand times! Her! Can't find the words any more! Again! let me look at her again! God, how beautiful she is! Enormous deep eyes! How languid in her movements . . . I could watch for ever. Want to touch! Want to hold!'

He seems to worship her, her fully dressed motions as she dances around in front of his eyes. Then she begins a very formal strip-tease:

'She seems to have bewitched the metals and heavy stones: not a clink! And now without bracelets her wrists reveal their whiteness! Her neck seems taller, more regal! . . . Now she's unhooked her dress and she's letting it slide over her hips down the shimmering silk. . . .'

Watching all this is such hot work that the grotesque client removes his own waistcoat and tie. But then, when she has nothing left on, the vision deepens with a Baudelairian intensity.

'What? You won't stop there? . . . . An animal shudder sharpens the outline of your nostrils, draws your cheeks in! Your eyes seem to withdraw into their deepening shadow! Your breast heaves more and more, faster and faster . . . the shiver that climbs from your ankles to your loins, from your wrists to your shoulders, ah! how it teases out the shape of you! You grow, you stretch, like a steel wand in fire. From the hollows of your eyes a bright stare transfixes me! Oh, my love, what's becoming of you? Your hips, shaken in waves of suffering, dislocate your lovely body! The light, which tended to your curves, now stabs angles into your body! Your knees, your shoulders—Pebbles! Knives! On the shield of your chest your ribs stand out like a sergeant's stripes.'

She still goes on stripping until he can see her bed through the empty cage of her ribs; and unable to stand any more, the client rushes at the door in a final moment of orgasmic horror and knocks himself stone-cold. The madame returns and says, 'I think the gentleman is satisfied'.

La Serrure makes a highly successful comment on vicarious sex, but it has essentially a verbal appeal—its interest is greater on the page or over the radio—than on the stage itself, where the problem of sustaining a long monologue of visual imagery is appallingly difficult. However, Tardieu's plays are ideal for lunch-hour or café theatre, where the constricted circumstances and the necessity for one or, at most, two actors, put a premium on short plays with a single strong idea.

FERNANDO ARRABAL, who was born in 1932 in what used to be Spanish Morocco, has been living in France since 1954. He writes in French, and his plays are immensely popular at the moment, especially in the United States. He is not dry and sardonic in the manner of Vian, or light and fantastical as Ionesco used to be. He is cruel, infantile, and in many ways crude: a Spanish surrealist who has a tremendous deal in common with his older compatriot, Salvador Dali. But he is by no means as substantial an artist as Dali.

He has invented something which he calls the Theatre of Panic. For instance: theatre is 'rite', 'ceremony', 'fête'—erotic, mystical, orgiastic, obscene, both 'temple and brothel'. When I saw *L'Architecte et l'empereur d'Assyrie* (The Architect and the Emperor of Assyria, 1967) at the Vieux-Colombier, in the celebrated Lavelli production, a leaflet was pushed into my hand announcing 'Panique'. Members of its ruling body included Pierre de Mandiargues, Olivier O. Olivier, Buñuel, César, Forest, and Paco Rabanne. In practice, Arrabal's theory boils down to a love of dressing up and childish outrage. The apocalyptic dialogue between Emperor and Architect turns out in many ways to be a kind of *Staircase* on a desert island; the two of them indulge in every bit of childish wish-fulfilment they can devise—a display of fetishism strictly *entre hommes*. They reverse roles, hang their braces on the crucifix, dress up skulls, beat and chain each other, and hack off with an axe their pedal extremities. The mother of one was eaten by a dog.

Arrabal has considerable vitality of dialogue, but he tends to squash his talent under his posturing. *L'Architecte et l'empereur* reminds one of far too many diverse influences. The two characters are a magpie quilt of Prospero and Caliban, Pozzo and Lucky, and they scratch about their cultural dungheap like mangy lords of the fleas. *Le Labyrinthe* (The Labyrinth, 1961) can be dismissed in even fewer words, but when it was recently done in Paris the production was erotic in the extreme (Jérome Savary was the director), and it caused a furore. Like other of Arrabal's plays, with the exception of the early and more formally comic *Pique-nique en campagne* (Picnic on the Battlefield, 1959) *Le Labyrinthe* has a promising theatrical idea which the posturing and provocative text does little to sustain. Savary's production tended to conceal it under an auditory storm of shouts, clucking noises, and whistles, confirming that Arrabal's mixture of myth and surrealism is better seen than listened to in detail.

In Savary's production the labyrinth itself was a maze of blankets, hung about the set, and all over the theatre, which had been transformed into a kind of environmental workshop. Half-naked characters even disappeared out of the theatre itself into the street, to confront amazed pedestrians. From the labyrinth the two main characters try to escape, and after the obligatory sexual rites and Barbarella fantasies, one of the two is accused of the murder of a third—who hanged himself from a lavatory cistern—and is condemned to death by a judge who wears knickers and a suspender belt, and presides from on top of a step-ladder at the back of the theatre.

It is a play for a director to take over and impose his own personality on. This is just what Savary—reportedly with amicable friction with the author—did. We had a matronly soprano with reassuringly perfect pitch singing 'waltzing, waltzing, high in the clouds,' between violent outbursts of heart-rending passion; there was one character who vomited with fast orgasmic frequency into a lavatory bowl, and while his nude form was hoisted upside down on a rope, a number of whirling maenads wove between the audience; a live goat also made an appearance. Apart from these elements, there was the stock-in-trade of the Arrabal shock-panic-cruelty: indecency, sacrilege, rape, nudity, crab-like dancing, and even nose-picking.

Le Cimetière des voitures (Car Graveyard, 1964) has an equally strong image at its centre, this time the car-wrecker's yard. The text is a better one than that of *Le Labyrinthe*, for it seems to be trying seriously to show a Christ-like figure, a trumpet player called Emanou, who wishes to play music to the souls of dead automobiles. But again, in production, the text takes a back seat. When I saw it, in Victor Garcia's unique and rightly famous production at the Théâtre des Arts, it was translated into a stunning visual myth of subconscious rampagings. One car was winched from the ceiling where it was suspended, and opened up, like the belly of some huge fish. Another was wheeled forward and a scene played in and out of its rusty doors. The display of nudity, violence, lights, and sonic effects was again at the forefront of the experience.

It is Arrabal's availability to the director's experimental fantasy, by his supply of some electric overriding image, to which much of his present success is due. In 1969 he was awarded the Prix de L'Humeur Noir; and in his most recent play, *Et Ils passèrent des menottes aux fleurs* (And They Put Handcuffs on the Flowers, directed by Arrabal in New York, 1972, and London, 1973), there is no evidence that his work is developing in the direction of sanity and discipline: the anal and sexual ceremonies proliferate, as ever, in their profanation of the Church, and their loving assertion of anarchy.

7 Dislocated consciousness

Estragon: (*hastily*) We're not from these parts, sir.
Pozzos: (*halting*) You are human beings none the less.

SAMUEL BECKETT (born 1906 in Dublin) is a classical artist, possibly the greatest of our day; he has had no romantic mission to accomplish: his works are, each of them, and taken all together, a sustained tractatus, a critique, a sceptical essay on man. The sceptical element is ignored, mostly because Beckett is thought of as a gallows-humoured Irish clown, the high priest of the absurd. His work is no more absurdist than the work of Genet: both are expressing a serious vision of life, which is to be taken entirely at its face value, a vision developed out of the raw matter of the artist's life and himself, a raw, literal, metaphor. It is by the quality of this vision that one is constantly affected in seeing and reading his plays, so that one is justified, in this chapter, in not dealing with specific works—either so well known as to need no further description or so brief and obscure as to defy analysis—but in attempting to offer some general conclusions as to its human and artistic power. Readers who require detailed critical evaluation of Beckett's plays should consult Eugene Webb's *The Plays of Samuel Beckett* (Peter Owen, 1973), John Fletcher and John Spurling's *Beckett: a study of his plays* (Eyre-Methuen, 1972), and essays edited by Melvin J. Friedman in *Samuel Beckett Now* (University of Chicago Press, 1970).

Beckett is an aesthetician of extraordinary power, whether he is describing the work of others, as in his book on Proust, as a translator, in his exquisite versions of Mexican poetry, or in the intensely descriptive introspections that constitute his novels. He is no moralist, and he is not concerned with the values of life as lived: Peter Brook has misunderstood him when he writes in *The Empty Space* that 'Beckett does not say "no" with satisfaction; he forges his merciless "no" out of a longing for "yes" and so his despair is the negative from which the contour of its opposite can be drawn.' This attitude can, however, easily be construed in performance of the plays, where an optimistic 'subtext' is suggested (as in Peter Hall's production of *Waiting for Godot*, Arts Theatre 1959, and Donald McWhinnie's production of *Endgame*, Aldwych 1965; it was not the case in Roger Blin's dark, original productions of both plays). But, in plays and novels alike, Beckett is simply saying 'no.' From time to time diminishing rays of a 'yes' may be projected, but they are quickly obliterated.

Beckett has worked in the reverse direction from Joyce. Joyce began writing narrative stories, with *Dubliners* and *Portrait of the Artist as a Young Man*, then, in *Ulysses*, he created a vast structure

51

of consciousness, a philological cathedral. *Finnegans Wake* is of an even greater elaboration and complexity: Joyce worked on nothing else for seventeen years—even the Sistine Chapel took Michelangelo only four. Joyce's linguistic and impenetrable joy bursts and overwhelms the considerations of narrative. Beckett has worked in reverse; his progress is a systematic *dépouillement*, a stripping bare. Both men are attracted by the rare, the obscure, the recherché.

It is significant also that both men should have lived in Paris: drying up in themselves fairly early the reciprocal processes of what is, or was, considered normal family life—patriotism, social involvement, material optimism, the education of children, by which an artist can go on taking from life and giving back to it. Exile seems to have induced two forms of concern in Beckett: one, a form of asceticism practised in his own life, the other an interest in an abstract, aesthetic process more similar to that of a painter or musician than a writer. Beckett differs radically from playwrights like Montherlant or Anouilh who find a form, and then develop through that form the variations of passion and idea that a changing and maturing life imprints on them. Beckett's work is a series of intuitions and impressions which realize what has been present in him all along, namely the flavour, the very essence, of himself.

All Beckett has written is the result of meticulous and conscious choice; never, possibly, has there been a writer who has been so self-conscious, so careful, so unprepared to give anything away, or to let himself go. His work is as much a process of self-concealment as of self-revelation. Beckett's self-concealment invites participation, but also asks you to ask him where he has gone. When he writes of Proust: 'the good or evil disposition of the object has neither reality nor significance. The immediate joys and sorrows of the body and the intelligence are so many superfoetations. Such as it was, it has been assimilated to the only world which has reality and significance, the world of our own latent consciousness, and its cosmography has suffered a dislocation. So that we are rather in the position of Tantalus, with this difference, that we allow ourselves to be tantalized'; he might have been writing about himself, his own future prose works and plays. (*Proust*, published in 1931, is, compared to the rest of his work, an enthusiastic tract on literature and perception.)

Hiding away, and the subsequent effect of tantalization, is the essence of Beckett and of his work. Myriad commentators and critics may see his work as an allegory on the end of civilization, but the same fatuous conclusions can be drawn from watching children at play, and new children go on being born every day. Beckett has learned the supreme skill of tantalization from his early influence, Joyce: both depend upon a highly sophisticated culture which is tempted into theorizing about their work, at the same time trying to recover its innocence. Martin Esslin's championing of the universal appeal of *Waiting for Godot* on the basis of a production before hardened criminals in St Quentin jail is typical of the critical attitude to Beckett. It is as dislocated as Peter Brook's reaction to Genet's *Les Nègres* (The Blacks, 1959)—in Paris it was 'baroque literary entertainment', in New York 'I am told the vibrations changed from night to night depending on the proportion of blacks to whites in the house.' Both attitudes are symptoms of an atavistic hunger, a craving that art should be as sensational as the newspaper headline.

Beckett is not very interested in being comprehended; no more interested than was Wittgenstein. He writes deliberately to be obscure, in its original meaning of devoid of light, gloomy, dismal, and the subject of his work is obscuration itself, the darkening or dimming of intellectual light, of the mental vision. He communicates this experience, and it is meant to be shared, not explained. There is nothing more to be said on the subject than he himself has said. It is even possible that popularity may have caused his later works, such as *Play, Breath* and *Not I*, to be more brief, more terminal, more delitescent; he has committed the sin of tantalization, and he is playing the consequences; he has complained of being 'sucked dry', on the 'sore subjects' of himself and his work; he has never liked critics. Indeed, there is no more abusive term in the language:

VLADIMIR: Sewer-rat!
ESTRAGON: Curate!
VLADIMIR: Cretin!
ESTRAGON: (*with finality*) Crritic!
VLADIMIR: Oh!
He wilts, vanquished, and turns away.

Dr Oliver Sachs in his remarkable book, *Awakenings*, dealing with the revival of long-standing Parkinsonian cases through the action of a miracle drug called El Dopa, quotes Donne's words: 'As sickness is the greatest misery, so the greatest misery of sickness is solitude . . . solitude is a torment which is not threatened in hell itself.' All the characters in Beckett's work are in solitude. But they are not in torment: they have passed beyond it, like frozen, numb statues, or indeed like the patients Dr Sachs describes with uncanny insight. To take but several of the pathological conditions Dr Sachs describes, there are:

Perseveration: a tendency to indefinite continuation, or repetition, of nervous processes—self-stimulating, self-reinforcing.
Hypokinesia: reduced force, impetus, or spread of movement.
Catalepsy: tireless, timeless, effortless maintenance of posture.
Festination: forced hurrying of speech.

These are strikingly akin to the behavioural characteristics of Beckett's characters, of Lucky in *Waiting for Godot*, of Hamm in *Endgame*, of Molloy, of Winnie in *Happy Days* (1961), or the anonymous compulsive Mouth of *Not I* (1973). Yet, in the theatre, there is nothing abstract in the realization of these states. Beckett's dislocated creatures are endowed with a classical simplicity and nakedness which has much in common with Jacques Copeau's approach to the art of acting. Copeau's influence was at its height just before and after the Second World War. An exercise in Copeau's school, which Etienne Decroux speaks of in *Paroles sur le mime*, consisted of playing 'sans paroles', the face covered over, the body practically naked, little plays of which 'a good number were sad'. They sound remarkably similar to Beckett's own mimes, *Act Without Words I* and *II* (1960).

Beckett brings a literal vision to life, a technically radiant translation of the picture he has formed of the spirit of man, of hell. It is an

inferno unredeemed by belief, or a counterbalancing vision of
heaven—unless we are prepared to set in the opposing scale the
melodious and deeply Catholic outpourings of the priestly poets of
Mexico upon which he has lavished such care and love. We can hardly set against

HAMM: Nature has forgotten us.
CLOV: There's no more nature.

the ecstasy of the passionate Manuel M. Flores:

The spotless world
was born in grandeur and serenity,
God looked upon creation
and saw that it was good.

(translated by Beckett in his
anthology of Mexican poetry)

But there is a connection: Beckett has created with his own work a
highly spiritual, and rarefied, parody of Western culture; parody is an
intellectual activity, not born of despair, but of wit and perception; of
ratiocination.

The loneliness expressed in Beckett is passionless: Hamm says in
Endgame 'Then babble, babble, words like the solitary child who
turns himself into children, two, three, so as to be together, and
whisper together, in the dark.' The paramountcy is one of mood, of
the degree of consciousness, of a passive state of feelings. For passion
there needs to be a subject and an object, there must be movement
between two elements. In *Godot* there is almost passion, a dramatic
continuity of mood, there are relationships. Since then Beckett has
moved increasingly into a world where the relationship between subject and object has broken down. There is a bitter, self-perpetuating
stasis. In *Proust*, Beckett propounds an aesthetic creed in which the
artist can only create by descending lower into himself, very much as
in Eliot's *Burnt Norton;* mystical illumination is achieved by a
lowering of consciousness:

Descend lower, descend only
Into the world of perpetual solitude,
World not world, but that which is not world,
Desiccation of the world of sense,
Evacuation of the world of fancy,
Inoperancy of the world of spirit;

In Beckett the symbolism is to be taken as real: the misery is
meant to be actual, and the only redeeming factor in human life is
habit.

CLOV: Why this farce, day after day?
HAMM: Routine.

The most difficult thing in life is to reorganize habit: this is
paralleled in Proust's *Les Intermittances du Cœur* (Beckett's *Proust*,
p. 4), in the narrator's second visit to Balbec, when this operation is
described as 'longer and more difficult than the turning inside out of
an eyelid, and which consists in the imposition of our own familiar
soul on the terrifying soul of our surroundings'.

Beckett is, as was Joyce, an impeccable craftsman, a master of the written word, a stylist whose only touchstone is himself. Beckett's nature is centred on solipsism. In *Godot, Endgame* and the novels, the sense of time is utterly personal: time is the monster of damnation and salvation. The novels are spiritual diaries, day-to-day rambling confessions from the masked, but none the less highly refined, sensibility of a 'decadent', an *émigré* Irishman: the sensibility is a deliberately cultivated one, redolent of *fin-de-siècle* humours, a Proust not of elegant drawing-rooms, but of rotting heaps of cabbages, of dog's urine and decaying faeces. Both Beckett and Proust share a strange obsession with smells, sensations, and above all, sounds or music.

For Beckett's characters the world is an old place: Vladimir says 'we should have thought of it when the world was young, in the nineties.' Beckett is a poet of mood from whom the philosophical virility of the French language has exacted a classical command and discipline. The redeeming grace of the pessimism is his truly prodigious technical art and power of literary evocation.

Sartre has talked about 'the solitude, the despair, the commonplaces of non-communication' as being 'profoundly and essentially bourgeois'. He has praised *Godot* as 'the play I find the best since 1945 . . . pessimistic, expressionistic . . . the kind of thing which appeals to the middle class'. Beckett has nothing to say for the future; recent plays such as *Not I* and *Breath* have become increasingly hermetic, a variation of focus on a vanishing point. As Joyce aged, his work ripened, became almost overblown; it sagged under linguistic elaboration. Beckett withers on the branch juiceless and shrivelled up, leaving exquisite late autumn colourings behind him: the essence of decay unspoilt by putrescence or sensuality. Perfect is the purity in every way save, possibly, in a refined but very consciously cultivated aestheticism. He has nothing to say because he has no concern with the future of man: as far as he is concerned, mankind is dead. 'Let me hear nothing of the moon, in my night there is no moon, and if it happens that I speak of the stars it is by mistake.' (*Molloy*)

Nature is one enormous still life, scraped, imprinted occasionally, with marks of the beast, or dusted with the light, hierographic tread of the spirit, or the silver, burnt-out slime of the affections. Nothing, possibly, dates so quickly as the eye watching its own power to record a dying vision. Generations to come seek vitality and future possibility, not deadness which can always be taken for granted as a condition of human existence. To find freshness and life we must turn to Beckett's early work, to *Murphy*, written when he lived for two years in London, in Edith Grove, to his inspired sermon on Proust, which is a *Religio Medici* of literature, to his lyrical and sensuous translations of Mexican poetry.

As for Beckett's plays, they create a strange and unique flavour, but they are only part of the truth. It is a dead end for a young child to play games of hiding and waiting, or who is master, who servant, for ever. The child must move on to its next stage of development—even if destructive—or wither. For all their extreme difference in most elements, the very young and the very old share one overriding factor in common: a submersion in unconscious psychic happenings.

8 Language and silence

'That appellation [theatre of the absurd] is itself absurd, because not one among them considers human life and the world as an absurdity. Certainly not Genet, who studies the *connection* of images and mirages, between themselves; nor Adamov, who is Marxist and who has written "no theatre without ideology".'

J.-P. Sartre

With Beckett, JEAN GENET (born 1910) is held to be the other undisputedly great dramatic and literary artist in France. It is well known that he has had numerous convictions for theft, and was serving a life sentence before he was freed because of an appeal by the country's leading intellectuals and artists to the President. His greatest admirer and apologist, Jean-Paul Sartre, has devoted a major work to a discussion of the significance of his life and attitudes (*Saint Genet: comédien et martyr*, 1952). When he was ten, Genet began stealing, and the harshness of his treatment at the hands of the authorities turned him from a perfectly behaved little boy, in Blake's terms, from an Angel into a Thief. Gradually, over the years, his dedicated larceny became hallowed with a kind of sanctity. He came personally, and with utter conviction, to embody the evil he saw in himself as an example to society, as an example to the vengeful authoritarian evil he saw society to be, to provoke it with his own naked honesty, to tempt it into retribution. It was society which had, in the first instance, turned him into a thief. He showed in his own life the 'eternal couple of the criminal and the saint'.

When he discovered statistics proving that roughly the same percentage of any society would be criminal, and when, also, in Barcelona, the police took him into custody and passed around a syringe of vaseline which he used in connection with his sexual needs, his beliefs underwent a metamorphosis. While they passed the object around, their disgust, and symbolically the disgust of all authority, was centred on the syringe instead of on him. He realized he need not be at the centre, and receiving end, of their ritualized hatred. He could produce something to take his place, some symbolic representation of himself, like the vaseline: namely a work of art.

A belief in art became central to his beliefs, as it is to Beckett's: simply by producing something, one is affirming something. But, specifically, Genet believes in the redeeming power of beauty with almost ecstatic fervour; 'to fight against the stubborn attention of his readers', Sartre wrote, 'to make them form thoughts which will repel them, there has to be a categorical imperative, constantly present in the words, and which is unconditionally adhered to. In brief, the work must be beautiful.'

So in Genet's plays, as in life, we have disgust constantly surmounted in a sense of beauty; the reader, or audience, loathes and identifies at the same moment. 'The sexual act itself is disgust surmounted.' Genet, when he throws himself into long excremental descriptions of anal coition, makes Sartre irresistibly 'call to mind Marie Alacogne licking up the festered droppings of the diseased.'

In the theatre, Genet has found the equivalent imagery to that of the metaphor and fantasy in his prose writings: in ceremonial, in dressing up, in repetition of action. He has also freed himself from his autobiographical obsessions, expanding into more social themes, such as the colour question in *Les Nègres* (1959) and the Algerian War in *Les Paravents* (The Screens, 1961).

But social content is only one of many surfaces. It is not the surface of reality that Genet is in any way concerned with. Leonardo da Vinci wrote in his notebooks that 'if two mirrors be placed so as to exactly face each other, the first will be reflected in the second, and the second in the first. Now the first being reflected in the second carries it to its own image together with all the images reflected in it.' Genet's characters reflect one another *ad infinitum*: Claire and Solange in *Les Bonnes* (The Maids, 1949) both envy and hate Madame, and dress up like her; Madame is not Madame, but a street-walker; the authoritarian figures in *Le Balcon* (The Balcony, 1960) play out their opposites as whores, thieves, liars, the blacks are whites in *Les Nègres*, and even Genet would have liked the characters in *Les Bonnes* to be played by men, to deepen a sense of image bouncing off a further reflector.

In the language of sexuality there is an ever-present sense of basic emotions, love, hate, greed, survival, breaking through elaborate social forms. But there is something passive about Genet's vision: it needs a commentator like Sartre to give it teeth, though the teeth he gives it in *Saint Genet: comédien et martyr* are often carious, and blackened with obscurity. The passivity is situated in Genet's sexuality, and in his conception of time. His homosexuality has been dealt with at prodigious length, first by himself, then by Sartre, and numerous others. It needs little further elaboration. Its recent influence is very strong in David Rudkin's play *Cries from Casement*, in which Casement's lonely vice with native boys is celebrated in rich and complicated imagery. But Genet's conception of time is the key to his obscure presentation of action.

'I know nothing very specific about time, but, if I acknowledge the existence and termination of an event, any event whatsoever, it seems that the present moment did not take place in a movement going toward the future, but that, on the contrary, the moment which is going to direct the event is no sooner born than culminates and flows back at top speed towards its birth, and settles upon itself.'

In other words, events have already happened, and even real life is only a playing back of the tape, or not even a playing back, merely a winding back in order to reach the beginning. And art, in all this, is but a shadow of a show: 'only a theatre of shadows can still touch me.' Since the formal qualities of the early plays, *Haute surveillance*

(Deathwatch, 1949) and *Les Bonnes*, the structure of the major works seems, deliberately, to collapse, fold in on itself.

Genet's theatre of shadows is a very platonic conception of the theatre, but it is not in any way lucidly expressed. He is entirely self-contradictory and instinctive. His view of his own work is that of an artistic megalomaniac. But his plays are successful not through their form, which is gauche, their symbolism, which is clumsy, their psy-chology, which is crude, but uniquely because he is a poet with an outstanding gift for words, and a rich ability to create, and celebrate in words a sensual and dominantly visual world. The appeal of his plays is in the language he uses, and Genet's fame amply demonstrates the primacy of the word in the French theatre. Genet may not love authority, or colonialism, or the police, but he loves the French language, and it receives as much homage from him in his use of its traditional structures, as from a government clerk carefully weighing his syntax in a department of justice.

Genet understands words; he writes with ecstasy and simplicity; he understands the tensions of the French language: he loves its paradoxes:

'The French language conceals and reveals a war of words, brotherly enemies, one snatching from the other or else falling in love with it. . . . French allows words to straddle each other like animals in heat, and what emerges from our mouths is an orgy of words . . .'

And these words strike with their greatest resonance on the inner eye. Genet always leaves us with a series of extraordinary visual im-ages, like Félicité's in *Les Nègres*.

'Regardez! Regardez! Madame. La nuit que vous réclamez la voici, et ses fils qui s'approchent. Ils lui font une escorte de crimes. Pour vous, le noir était la couleur des curés, des croque-morts et des orphelins. Mais tout change. Ce qui est doux, bon, aimable et tendre sera noir. Le lait sera noir, le sucre, le riz, le ciel, les colombes, l'espérance, seront noirs—l'opéra aussi, où nous irons, noires, dans des Rolls noires, saluer des rois noirs, entendre une musique de cuivre sous les lustres de cristal noir . . .'

There is the young and beautiful thief in *Le Balcon*, her breasts bare, being whipped by the executioner, or, in more detail, in *Les Paravents*, the mother in her hair of tow, a white face, made up with cerise and very elaborate wrinkles—blue, mauve, purple—from the eyes to the temples, 'from the wings of the nose to the mouth and down around the chin'; the spectacle of Claire and Solange in *Les Bonnes* dominating and being abused in turn, but first and foremost with pictures, with ceremony for the eye, with visual ritual:

SOLANGE: And you were going to follow in the wake of the boats, to cross the sea to aid and comfort your handsome exile! Look at yourself again! That role is only for the fairest of the fair. The guards would snigger. People would point at you.

All this succession of images and mirages shows how strongly Genet would agree with the author of Ecclesiastes that all was vani-ty. The reflections in Genet's case are curiously sick, distorted, and meant to disturb. But unravel all the diabolical distortions, and one may find God: a belief in pure evil is as much an assertion as a belief in pure good.

Genet remains very much the unrepentant sinner. To take away from him his sense of sin would be the same as removing whisky from the desperate alcoholic, or heroin from the addict. Genet is drugged with a fantasy of universal evil.

The novelist MARGUERITE DURAS (born in Indochina in 1904) has expanded and developed her dramatic talent since her first play, *Le Square* (1956), was performed at the Studio des Champs-Elysées. After Genet, Duras reads like a wistful and feminine 'post coïtum tristitia'.

Le Square is a duologue between a middle-aged man and a young girl. It captures the essence of loneliness, of silence, and graspings towards communication.

La Musica (1965) and *Les Eaux et les forêts* (The Waters and the Forests, 1965), are very successful evocations in the same manner as *Le Square*, but they have nothing new to add to this early master-piece. In *Yes, Peut-être* (1967), and *Le Shaga* (1967), Duras takes a step backwards, into more rarified self-conscious and literary texts. The first, *Yes, Peut-être*, opens on a bare white set: two women in uniform drag on a wounded soldier; he has the name 'Patrice' scrawled over his denim blouse. The action takes place in the future, after the very last war of all has been fought; another theatrical response to the Vietnam war, but without the interior quality of Duras' best dialogue, it deteriorates into endless weak word games and repetitions of 'Yes, Yes'. *Le Shaga* is merely a conversation piece, written largely in an invented language.

L'Amante anglaise (A Place without Doors, or, The Lovers of Viorne, 1968) suffers, as do all interrogatory plays when the victim and the criminal are known in the first few minutes, from a lack of progression. Although the murder committed by Claire Lannes of her cousin, Marie-Thérèse, is an especially horrifying one, and is based on a true story, Duras' treatment is on the same level of fantasy and non-communication as her other work. It is a model of suc-cinctness and simplicity. Everything is dead about the murderess Claire, her emotions are dead, her desires are dead, her intellect is dead. The play is a complete exploration of this woman's remote and lonely life, slowed down not only by time, but by the interrogator, a sensible and humane seeker after truth. The investing of the facts of crime with Duras' strangely unreal and fascinating question-and-answer technique makes one ask whether she chose the right story for her talents. The gruesome village event and the delicate sensibili-ty of Duras are not convincing together for one reason only; because Duras is a very romantic writer, and there is no romantic notion about this crime that can be established. It belongs to the fixed percentage of criminal behaviour which helped to deflate Genet's sense of heroic criminal superiority. However, with Madeleine Renaud playing Claire, it emerged as an extraordinary *tour de force*, claimed by some as a masterpiece.

It is with *Suzanna Andler* (1971) that Duras' talents have found their richest embodiment to date. *Suzanna Andler* is a study of that particular kind of ennui which attaches to a young-to-middle-aged, rich, French woman who can afford to pay a million francs to rent a villa in St Tropez during August. It takes place one winter's day in the villa Suzanna Andler is considering at that price. With a classic simplicity, and Duras' usual but extraordinarily discreet disregard for a story, there are but four characters, four duologues, and one telephone call.

The 'phone call in *Suzanna Adler* is a classic example of a strong theatrical convention. A whole book could be written about the use of telephone calls in French literature, from Proust's narrator's call to his grandmother, to Cocteau's *Voix humaine* (The Human Voice, which Beckett has called 'an unnecessary banality') and Roger Vitrac and René de Obaldia, who both make much use of the telephone in *Médor* and *L'Air du large*. The call to Suzanna is expected for much of the play, and comes through just after the interval: it is from Suzanna's husband, Jean, who is in Chantilly, presumably with one of his many mistresses. Jean has had many affairs, never discussed between them. Suzanna has been more faithful: at last she has taken a lover, but it is her very first. He is accompanying her on the villa-hunt. It is when the estate agent has departed, and Suzanna's ennui has carried her off into a sleep that lasts several hours, that her lover arrives. Later, in their second dialogue, after a meeting with her husband's ex-mistress (by means of whom she explores her knowledge of her husband), she is told by her lover that she always looks about to die or fall asleep; by the end, some love does seem to have been kindled.

There is the same inward stillness in the dialogue as there was in *Le Square*: a strangely absorbing quality, the effect is slightly disturbing, immensely demanding of attention, and ultimately very evocative: similar, in many ways, to the songs of Debussy, which imitate the processes of nature with impressionistic ambiguity. Duras does something of the same kind of thing with the thoughts and love processes of the affluent. Often Suzanna remains locked in the inexpressible; then suddenly a feeling, a buried desire, a crushed hope, a recognition, breaks to the surface. The effect is haunting.

The romanticism is allowed full expression in Duras' latest work, *India Song* (1973), commissioned by the English National Theatre. In it, Duras returns to the themes of earlier work, of her film scripts *Hiroshima mon amour*, and *Moderato cantabile*. *India Song*, which has yet to be seen on the stage, is a love story of the 1930s, set on the banks of the Ganges, told by a number of anonymous voices, some male, some female.

Like *L'Amante anglaise*, there is an absorption in mood which is effective, but there is not the positive and concrete image, as is provided by the villa itself in *Suzanna Andler*, or was provided in *Hiroshima* by film of the devastated city. *The Square* and *Suzanna Andler* have very definite locations: *India Song*, for all its potent evocativeness, seems to unfold only on a band of light, where colours, love-making, shadows, play in fascinating harmony and progression, and on a band of sound, where voices converse with all the mastery of one of the foremost writers of dialogue in our age. These elements do not create an image which is primarily theatrical, but an image which still needs a stronger sense of the objective correlative for the mood or fantasy, be it of love or of death, the implications of which Duras can evoke with such delicate nuance. Well may it be, as Duras has written, a story of love 'immobilized in the culmination of passion'. But there is little drama in being immobilized on a high plateau, unless chasms and abysses are also revealed from time to time.

9 Jeunes auteurs (I)

'Let us not then speak ill of our generation, it is not any unhappier than its predecessors.'

Samuel Beckett

In this chapter I propose to discuss the work and importance of some lesser known figures in the French theatre. The playwright's profession is particularly difficult in France except for those several distinguished and fortunate individuals whose fame has made them financially independent. The playwrights known as 'jeunes auteurs' literally 'young'—are those who are not yet generally known; so naturally enough there are plenty of 'jeunes' who are getting on in years. I have, in Chapter 1 p. 1, mentioned the meeting of playwrights organized in 1969 by Jean-Pierre Miguer which fifty or so playwrights attended. The Society of Playwrights has roughly 15,000 members but many of these are involved in film, radio, and television. And indeed, when people complain about the lack of new playwrights, what they often mean is that the directors have not the time to read any new work which is submitted to them. Few of the heavily subsidized theatres perform the work of new playwrights, and those who manage to have their plays presented owe it as much to their obstinacy and their powers of endurance as to their inherent talent. Even those who succeed in achieving a production of their plays are frequently disappointed, for they cannot hope for more than twenty or so performances, and with a cut of the royalties at 13 per cent of the gross receipts, they generally earn very little—in the subsidized theatres, prices of seats are relatively low. In addition, it is very unlikely that the play will be revived by another group before ten years have passed. There are few examples, Mlle Rozental claims in her *Notes et Etudes*, of new plays which have been presented in a commercial theatre. The tax situation makes it essential for each new production there to originate at the theatre itself, instead of being transferred from a provincial theatre, as often happens on this side of the Channel. The most certain way, therefore, a playwright can hope to make money is to sell his work abroad. This sometimes happens (in early 1974 J-L. Grumberg's *Dreyfus* was sold to a Broadway producer for 18,000 dollars), but unless a play is successful in Paris, it has little chance of performance in other countries.

Commercial theatre is, naturally enough, obsessed by the problem of profit; as little risk as possible is taken in order to break even; a success brings a big return, but it is the exception, and from then on the author is besieged with requests, more or less openly, to back any new work he might produce—although this is formally forbidden by the Society of Playwrights. But nothing stops the playwright trying to raise money to put on his plays, or from using a pseudonym, if he has money of his own. Unfortunately, the majority are without any money and this is for numerous directors sufficient reason not to read their manuscripts.

If the author has no money, the next most promising way is to use a star. From the director's point of view the author who can supply both is the ideal. But for the most part the commercial theatres in Paris, like those in London and New York, fall back on playing as safe as they possibly can, using the time-worn recipes of marital intrigue, sex comedy, and thriller. Examples of these are legion, and the most skilful more than justify their success, and in some cases, international fame. Many of the following, for instance, have been widely and frequently performed throughout the world: André Roussin's *La petite Hutte* (The Little Hut, 1947), Marcel Achard's *Patate* ('Tater', 1957), Félicien Marceau's *L'Œuf* (The Egg, 1956) and *La bonne Soupe* (The Good Soup, 1958), François Billetdoux's *Tchin-tchin* (1959), Françoise Sagan's *Un Château en Suède* (A Castle in Sweden, 1960) Barillet and Grédy's *Fleur de cactus* (Cactus Flower, 1964), Marcel Mithois' *Croque-Monsieur* (1964), Marc Camoletti's *Boeing-Boeing* (1969). In recent years there has been an invasion of Anglo-Saxon nudity shows. Even so, there are still certain theatres called 'theatres of research' which do try out new work—though they grow fewer and fewer. As far as I know there is only one play-writing competition, which is run by the Casino of Enghien: the first prize is for 10,000F., and there are three other prizes, each of 5,000F.

PHILIPPE ADRIEN was born in 1939, and his first profession was acting; he has not written much for films or television, and several of his plays are still in manuscript. *En Passant par la Lorraine* (Going through Lorraine) was written in 1968 and performed at the Comédie de Bourges, the Théâtre de Poche, and the Grenier de Toulouse. *La Baye* which was done first at the Centre Dramatique National du Sud-Est and then at the Avignon Festival, and finally at the TNP in Paris, has attracted most attention to date: it has been performed in Berlin, Frankfurt, and Madrid.

Adrien considers the normal conditions of show business very constricting, and despises the criteria of what he calls 'beauty, laughter, perfection, culture, etc.' He opts for the 'alternative' idea of group theatre which he thinks fulfils a need for liberation from the shackles of commercial interest and profit. His enthusiastic ideas stem largely from Sartre with their concern for the contradictions at the heart of society and of man, and the need for a 'prise de conscience'. But he is clearly, as are some young English writers, very interested in group theatre, and group evolution of new work. 'The most urgent question' he writes, 'concerns the functioning of the group itself and the relationships between its members.'

His practice, judging from *La Baye*, is very different from his theory, and it is to be hoped that the positive talent he shows in this play is not going to be placed in jeopardy by his theoretical concerns. *La Baye* (The Bay, 1967) is basically a family comedy which skates thinly over the theatre of the absurd, prodding and chipping here and there a little deeper. There are two families shown in it: in the first half, the Louis family is presented—Louis, Louise, Petit-Louis, Louisette, Gros-Louis, and so on. They play out among themselves a series of family quarrels, in a well established routine of repetitious chastisement. The comedy is amplified by chutes and ladders descending from the windows of an exterior setting, as well as a whistling and exploding kitchen range wittily constructed within it.

Family one, the Louis, are preparing for the arrival of family two, the Jeans; duly, after falsely raised hopes, they actually make their appearance. Holding up their arrival, however, is a weakness on Adrien's part, for having maintained one's expectations for the Jeans rather well, particularly through the hysteria of the mother, Louise, he inexplicably throws one's hopes of further expectation away on one of the children's jokes. He does not then quite have the skill to remount the excitement, so that when the Jeans do arrive the comic impact is slight.

La Baye hardly slackens a moment in its vitality, however, and is at its best in the furious clash of cordialities between the two families. Every twist of hilarious pain is wrenched from the aggressive exchange of manners as the two families settle down to eat their soup, facing out in a wide arc to the bay itself, a nostalgic point of rest to which both families continually return. A further development, or arrival, is that of the eldest son, Jean-Louis. New arrivals, in absurd drama, often substitute for old-fashioned development, again underlining the preoccupation with the deracination mentioned in Chapter 5. It may well owe something to the mass movement and unprooting of populations during the second World War: seen in this light, *Waiting for Godot* is the very essence of the drama of arrival anxiety.

In *La Baye* Jean-Louis arrives unheralded, down the chute, and the play is never clear as to which family spawned him. He is a soldier, and he falls suddenly in love with Louisette. But he has to go off and fight in the war; Grand Jean, the grandfather, dies, and the play winds up on a note of optimistic uncertainty. The two youngest sons of the rival families, perched high on the cloister battlements overlooking the bay, make an alternate refrain of 'Peut-être . . . peut-être un jour . . . peut-être . . .' Although this ending is effective, before we arrive at it Adrien seems to be pushing too hard towards a resolution; the soldier's arrival has little to do with what has gone before, it could have been positively contradictory; the mixing of absurdist and sentimental techniques seems to catch the playwright on the wrong foot.

La Baye's deep originality is to be doubted. It is not nearly as good a play as Romain Weingarten's *L'Eté*, which marries the absurd and sentimental elements with greater harmony, and gives evidence of a deeper observation. Its social animus has something in common with Brecht's *The Lower Middle-Class Wedding Party*, although Brecht's ironic and savage delight is missing. The linguistic model for *La Baye* is certainly Ionesco, but it is an Ionesco toned down, exploited and served to the masses without his fastidious logic and desperate rhythms.

Yet it is very good fun: the Gallic obsession with eating and drinking, combined with punning, is generally good theatrical fare; exaggerated manners never tire if they have a touch of Rabelaisian humour. The spontaneity, the often coarse anarchy of the language, have a rollicking irresistible force. It is a pity that Adrien should want to submit his personal gift to the levelling tendency of group creation, because the power of group activity in creating something new or exciting generally only comes about when the group is dominated or developed by an especially strong individual, as in the case of Ariane Mnouchkine, or Joan Littlewood.

LILIANE ATLAN is a new writer in another tradition, that of the social or historical documentary, like Planchon, Vinaver, or Jean Cosmos. She is known by one play, *Monsieur Fugue, ou Le Mal de terre* (1966) which was performed at the TNP, in their new Salle Gémier, named after Firmin Gémier, 1869–1933, who created the role of Father Ubu in 1896. The theme is directly recognizable and historical: a lorry-load of Jewish children is being driven to the gas chambers by the Nazis. They are accompanied by another prisoner, a former Nazi who has unexpectedly renounced his party and become more human—he is the Monsieur Fugue of the title—and with him the children act out a succession of savage scenes. As the moment of death grows nearer they become more conscious of life—until they have attained purity and dignity.

The violence with which this idea finds expression, it could be claimed, is worked up to an excessively hysterical pitch. Saturation point with the children screaming at each other is reached too quickly. But, in spite of this, the shuttling of scenes between the front and back of the lorry is an original device.

VICTOR HAÏM is one of the most talented of the new French playwrights. He was born in 1935 and attended the Conservatoire at Nantes before going to Paris; after working for Citroën and serving in the army, he joined various professional journals. His first play called *Mourir en chantant*, which he wrote in 1958, was read in 1966 by Pierre Valde who presented it at the Théâtre de Colombes, where Bertrand Poirot-Delpech, at that time critic of *Le Monde*, praised it warmly. Haïm was encouraged by this and quickly wrote *L'Arme blanche*, which is about the war in Vietnam. This was at the time when plays about Vietnam such as Peter Brook's *US*, or Armand Gatti's *V comme Vietnam* were much in vogue. Haïm's *L'Arme blanche* (Side-arm) is, however, by far the most striking of the anti-war plays, and on the strength of its reception Haïm left his job and has since, not without great material difficulty, devoted himself to writing for the theatre. *L'Arme blanche* has been performed in Austria and Sweden, and the rights were acquired by the Royal Shakespeare Company and other foreign companies. It is a great pity it was never presented in England, for Haïm has managed to achieve a very straightforward and simple treatment of the subject with a cast of only six, no scenic disturbances, no computers, no napalm, and no newsreel.

L'Arme blanche is the story of Stephen Humphrey, who 'volunteers' for a foreign war against the wishes of his mother, though very much in accordance with those of his father and the local mayor who is an ingratiating household fixture. The first part of the play portrays the agony of the mother's opposition to his going, and her violent conflict with her husband's conforming patriotism. Written and conceived with passion and clarity, it has the strong bold emotional flavour of early O'Neill; the mayor's *bonhomie* is an ultimatum, and the boy has to go; the one childish fear he expresses is that 'out there' the enemy trains vultures to kill and flies them at sentries.

In the second part the jolly mayor comes to announce that Stephen is being sent home. Although not wounded, as his mother has feared, he has developed a rather odd attachment to a vulture he has trained, and he is considered slightly mad. But he is a hero—he has been in the war long enough to qualify as that. So, with the vulture on his shoulder, he arrives home deeply changed, and he is determined to tell of his experiences. The mayor turns up to welcome him and, although he has a supper engagement, he is kept listening to Stephen's experiences by the menace of the trained vulture perched outside his door, ready to obey his master's wishes. By a swift transference, the vulture, an Ibsenesque symbol in the first act, becomes a dramatic agent in the action of the second. Stephen makes his grandparents, his parents, and the mayor participate in his war stories. Flatly and without pity he forces them into their horror roles, turning the mayor into a village elder who was kicked to death, and a soldier who was castrated in a brothel. He directs, as well as acts, in a scene in which his mother takes the part of a street-walker who is fought over by father and son. Finally the grandmother, mayor and father are bombed by grandfather, who tears about the room in his wheelchair, arms planing and tossing fruit out of a basket.

Then, in a touch worthy of the best moments of Arden's *Sergeant Musgrave's Dance*, Stephen reveals the true intention of his return—to bring revenge upon those who are the war's true cause, father, grandfather, mayor. Leaving the house with his mother, he abandons them to the vulture who, with spreading wings, looms over all of them in a destructive embracing shadow as the final moments fall.

As Haïm was himself in Algeria for fourteen months, one assumes the real experience behind the play's impact was the Algerian war, and that he has brought it up to date with Vietnam. The situations are neither propagandist, nor forced to shock or impress; they are outside the fashionable projections of conscience that self-congratulatory intellectuals like to practise, not only in France. It is a play about the dilemma and effects of war, and it is a very brave play to have written at this present time, as the method is so personal and vulnerable. Haïm modestly points out in the play's introduction that 'the forms presented in a certain kind of theatre—that of documentation or agitation—have not always given effective results.' On the other hand he admits that 'the slightest image of an actual event projected for four seconds, watch in hand, is a hundred times, a thousand times, more violent than a text, than situations developed on the stage itself.' Knowing the risks he is taking, he achieves success primarily because he has a marvellously sure grasp of dialogue. He knows just how far to go in his treatment of character; though they could easily be caricatures, the father and the mayor emerge as real and well-rounded people.

Victor Haïm has been unlucky in the quality of some productions of his plays (that of *L'Arme blanche* was poor) as well as in their frequency. J. L. GRUMBERG (born 1939) has been more fortunate. His *Dreyfus* (1974) had a far more successful production at the Théâtre de L'Odéon, though it is by no means as strong and original a play as *L'Arme blanche*. *Dreyfus* is set in Poland in 1930, and tells the story of a group of Jews who are rehearsing a play about the celebrated Dreyfus case: they dispute among themselves their own problems of being Jewish, they are involved in a fight with two Jew-baiters, their own lives and relationships penetrate the half-mythical story of persecution which they are trying to present. Grumberg, who was born in 1939, first came to be noticed with his adaptation of Chekhov's *The Duel*. His *Amorphe d'Ottenburg* is a more ominous and symbolic piece in which a prince, who is a homicidal monster comically endowed with the inability even to pronounce his own name without a terrible stammer, mercilessly puts to death everyone he considers to be useless. It is a strange uncompromising work, far less human than *Dreyfus*, which has a more realistic and compassionate atmosphere. The rhythm of *Dreyfus* is more that of a popular Jewish play, with its frequent digressions into long religious or idealistic statements, its sudden outbursts of violence, or its quick and lively sections of family or sentimental conflict. But conforming to the political philosophy of the majority of young writers, *Dreyfus* also looks forward to the future, as can be seen from the letter which Maurice, one of the cast who has left the rehearsals, writes to the others:

'I've thought a lot about you all and what you want to do together with Dreyfus ... I believe we were, and it was my fault, on the wrong track ... The man of today whether he's an artist or a worker, mustn't concern himself with the past, he must turn towards the future, he must construct the future ... Here, in Warsaw, I'm working in a large factory, I'm no longer living in an exclusively Jewish world, I'm a man among other men, a worker among other workers. I've been lucky enough to meet up with some members of the Polish Communist party, many of them Jewish—not that it's important to them or to the others, who are not—and we've talked much about all kinds of things, including you, my friends, and they've opened my eyes. To beat anti-semitism and all other forms of discrimination and oppression it's enough to change the actual structure of society: the rest will follow. When capitalism is beaten, communism will illuminate the world and liberate all men, this is the aim, this is the struggle ... Immense, beyond measurement, impossible, you say? But if it's true that David beat Goliath, who can resist the millions of Davids joined together as brothers and struggling together in order to change the world of tomorrow?

'As you can see I'm far away from the theatre and from art in general, but patience—everything in its own good time.'

It may read like Clifford Odets' *Waiting for Lefty*, or Arnold Wesker's *Chicken Soup with Barley*, yet in picking the year of 1931 to set *Dreyfus*, Grumberg has chosen a period of great change and social mobility where issues were very confused, where community life was breaking down, as it does among this group of Jews. Thus the historical parallel with today is very striking.

10 Jeunes auteurs (2)

‘ "Malraux, bourgeois culture, the Théâtre de France, Barrault, the whole lot has got it coming: all that is finished! Zero! annulled! suppressed! killed!'

Madeleine and I, sitting on the floor side by side, asked our neighbours who the young gentleman was.

"Cohn-Bendit?"

"ah! . . . the famous . . . oho!"

I remembered him from two years before, when he had laid above him in defence of *Les Paravents*. My 'old' education, composed of surrealist humour, came back into my head. People were looking at us. They asked me to reply. With the same insolent irony, only using courtesy instead of insults, I did so, and concluded with:

"All right! Barrault is dead, but there remains facing you a living creature. . . ." '

Jean-Louis Barrault (translated by Jonathan Griffin)

RENÉ EHNI (born 1935) made a brilliant début as a playwright with *Que ferez-vous en novembre?* (What will you be doing in November?) at the Théâtre Lutèce in 1968, just after the student uprisings of May. Since then he has written only one play—for television (*Eugénie Kopronime*). Ehni is an excellent satirist of political attitudes, an equivalent to Trevor Griffith who wrote *The Party*, performed at the British National Theatre. In both plays the characters sit around and discuss revolution, the only strong difference being that in Ehni's play the events had just happened, while in Griffith's play they are referred back to by enlarged newsreel photographs.

Curiously enough *Que ferez-vous en novembre?* was actually written before the events that conferred importance on it, and indeed confirmed that it had prophetic foresight. It is a rambling feast, as well as a considerable feat, of talk. A group of intellectuals are on holiday in Normandy, and, in the style of Plato's *Symposium*, during a day of eating—the action, if it can be described as such, takes place within the unities of time and place—they chat through the never-never land of revolutionary idealism. At the same time they give us sidelong glances at their pasts, their hearts and that Gallic *sine qua non*, their gastronomical fantasies.

Food is an ironically enforced theme from the very beginning. It immediately creates an irritation which, dramatically, is of great profit. The oldest of the three men in the play, Edward One, aged 40, used to be a member of the resistance; Edward Two, ten years younger, helped to 'pacify' Algeria, in the Orwellian double-think phraseology current at the time. Urs, at 20, has his revolutionary zeal still intact. Edward One declares, first thing in the morning, that he cannot smoke before eating, and cannot listen to the radio before coffee. Later, Edward Two, who has been seeking free-range eggs with Edward One's wife, Généreuse—insisting they should come from a hen fertilized by a particularly virile cock—takes off into an imaginative flight over butter (the very best, in which one can taste the smell of fresh grass) and home-made jam, claiming he will grow fatter and fatter: 'when war breaks out I'll be so bloated I'll fly around like a Zeppelin, I'll float above the mushrooms like a paunchy old papa.'

Food plays a part, too, in dreams of a future, and they soon find themselves discussing the 'plat du jour' of the communistic dream, which is to be a 'méchoui', a word from the Algerian, meaning a sheep roasted whole. The young man, Urs, says contemptuously that all the others can ever think about is eating. 'Very true' replies Edward Two, 'they sat us down round a table at the liberation, and we've been stuffing ourselves ever since.' We are firmly in the tradition of Marie Antoinette's famous 'let them eat cake', which 1968 gossip attributed to General de Gaulle in the form of a retort to the students: 'Let them eat chaos.'

Apart from the insidious gastronomical undercurrent there are other touches in Ehni's play to fill out the picture of revolutionary inertia. Edward One, in a profoundly moving speech, exhorts the young hothead Urs to take himself off to Bolivia, explaining that he himself is too old. There are outbursts of satirical disillusionment against the French left:

ED ONE: The French left, I ask you! Harking back to the time when it dreamed of its paratroops. Never pure enough, the 'para', never left-wing enough, however sweet, however seductive. But somehow it never clicked. Then there was Bigeard . . . But with the Israeli parachutist it was different. They rushed to baptize him 'para of the left'. At last, ta-ta-tum, no shame! Blond with blue eyes, with an irresistible schoolboy smile, we find him sitting beside the canal in a wicker chair . . . it gives me the shivers . . . I've come across him in *Paris-Match*, in *L'Express*, in *Christian Witness*. He's made the cover story of the *Nouvel-Observateur*, and at one moment it was even a question of publishing his picture in *Le Monde*—unheard of, but once needn't be a habit—so seductive he was. It's not everyday the left has such appeal . . .

To this speech, Ed Two replies 'I've finally got my hands on a good wine merchant in Paris.'

Urs leaves but doesn't go to Bolivia. The others construct a heroic picture around his departure, but it turns out that Urs has merely driven off to the Côte d'Azur with some Alsatian girls in a Peugeot 404 'décapotable'. The gesture—even the emotion behind it—is all the time tempered by the irony of the material circumstances. It is not so much that they do not want to do something, but that modern life has just become too big. *Que ferez-vous* abounds in images of the scientific age eroding nature and individualism—even the Communist party has become a frivolity and an indulgence.

For Ehni it is progress which is the true enemy. The French may make a new revolution like the student revolution but it took place more in the minds and imaginations of the students and public than in any real sense. Revolution is just another twentieth-century product, it is a revolution on paper, a revolution of publicity and newsreel coverage. The pressure is such that the real violence has no reality, the real issues no chance against basic appetites now more fully gratified than at any other point in time. Even liberty itself is part of the conspiracy: 'to come back to the question of our liberty' says Ed Two, 'the fact that everything can be said, everything printed, proves nothing about the degree of liberty we've actually got. Removing the teeth from ideas is one of capitalism's most remarkable successes. You tell me, if you can, an idea which will stand beside a superb car, a superb skyscraper, a superb bomb, or a superb motorway—I bet you can't.'

Que ferez-vous is one of the most extraordinary plays to have been written in France for some time: many writers just then were thinking of trying to write that kind of play. The freshness of Ehni's approach was that he had no inhibitions about putting highly articulate people on the stage and letting them express their thoughts. It is a practice that has been much followed since then, in France itself and elsewhere, though never quite to such honest and good effect.

In taking one playwright from the absurdist school, one from the social realist, committed stratum, and one straightforwardly satirical commentator, I have touched on the variety of 'jeunes auteurs'. There are others well worthy of consideration. I have spoken of Arrabal, Weingarten, Michel, Césaire, and Marguerite Duras in other chapters. In the footsteps of the committed left-wingers like Armand Gatti is GABRIEL COUSIN, who used to be a sports teacher, and who has written *L'Aboyeuse et l'automate* (The Barker and the Automaton), *Cycle du crabe* (Crab Cycle, 1968), *Le Drame du Fukuryu-Maru* (1963) which Gérard Philipe would have presented in 1960 at the TNP had he not died, and *L'Opéra noir*. All deal with contemporary themes, urgent political situations like guerilla uprising (*Cycle du crabe*), the sterility and disfigurement in the wake of atomic war (*Fukuryu-Maru*), or the racial question (*L'Opéra noir*). Cousin has stated that his aim is to show that 'misery, injustice, and war are not inevitable', and that he wishes 'to sow concern in the consciences of others. I have no wish to impose, and I don't want to prove anything.'

ANDRÉ BENEDETTO (born 1931) is another playwright of a decidedly political bent whose works, *Statues* (1966), *Napalm* (1967), *Lola pelican* (1968), *Zone rouge* (1968), *Auguste et Peter* (1968) and *Le Petit train de monsieur Kamode* (1969) have all been performed by the Nouvelle Compagnie d'Avignon. A project in which he was involved in 1970 was a collective effort of playwriting which became known as *Emballage* (Packaging). He was invited by the Maison de la Culture of Le Havre to write a play about the working conditions in this flourishing port town. He wrote to the trade union representatives and advertised for any one else to come forward and help him who wished to, and claimed that all he did in the work was to gather together the various threads, and present as objectively as he could all he had seen and heard.

The result would have pleased Sartre, who has called for a greater representation of work in the theatre. It showed also what a considerable influence Arnold Wesker's *The Kitchen*, performed by Ariane Mnouchkine's group theatre, Le Théâtre du Soleil, has had both on collective work and social themes. When *The Kitchen* opened at the Cirque de Montmartre in 1968 it not only made Wesker the most popular foreign dramatist in France, but it opened the way for the local treatment of innumerable work themes. Curiously enough, the experience which led Wesker to write *The Kitchen* was a French one—he worked as a pâtissier in a French restaurant for nine months—so when it was adapted by Philippe Léotard into French, the Parisian equivalents were authentic.

But *Emballage* by no means possesses the lively naturalistic flair of *The Kitchen*. Benedetto takes as his main character a nobody called Alexandre Zacharie, who finds a fresh fish on a Le Havre quayside, and decides he wants to eat it. Realizing he needs money, and he has no inherited wealth, and rejecting thievery and lying, he sees that work is the only way. Several workers in Le Havre give him a picture of work conditions, and he can almost see himself among them. Then he becomes prey to the tentacles of publicity, and he dreams of owning a motor-car. He lets himself easily be talked into signing on by a capitalist, and at the end of the day's work, worn out, he hasn't earned enough to buy the fish that tempted him in the first place. So he dreams of a Marxist future.

It sounds very simplistic: few workers today could work a whole day without earning enough to buy a fish. But just as Christian dramas used to take Biblical texts as their basis—Jesuit dramas in the sixteenth century in particular had an unconcealed didactic purpose, and were performed in public places, sometimes taking three days and with 300 people performing in them—so Benedetto's play bases its authority on Marx's writings. Marx wrote (in *Economic and Political Manuscripts*) 'Production does not only produce man as a *commodity*, the *human commodity*, man in the form of *commodity*; in conformity with this situation it produces him as a *mentally* and *physically* dehumanized being.'

When Alexandre Zacharie meets a student on the quayside, the student is determined to sermonize on the fish.

STUDENT: One moment. . .
    Man doesn't live by fish alone
    Listen to my words: I'm going to explain . . .
    You have unveiled the great secret
    Which is hidden in the fish: it's man.
    Which is hidden in all goods for sale: it's man.
    I have discovered to you there even what Aristotle himself
    Never discovered
    Have a good look . . .

The didacticism is simple and strong, though not necessarily based on accuracy. According to Marx, Aristotle had already seen the exchange of commodities as something that was extremely enigmatic. But Benedetto is right in so far as Aristotle failed to see the common factor of human labour in all goods. Later, in the same scene between the student and Zacharie, the fish is packaged by the student.

> Either you catch it yourself with your work,
> Or you pay those who catch it for their work!
> Now the demonstration is over.
> I close the fish and I send it along
> To its nest of brown seaweed in a special package
> Studied to make the buyer salivate at the forms
>   and the colours.
> I cunningly knot the string and the sale begins
> of this commodity which has not come to market
> on its own paws! Any takers?

ALEXANDRE(*holding out his hand*): I'll take it!
BERTHE(*shouting from a distance*): Take it!
THE MERCHANT (*coming in between*): Hands off! One moment—That fish is mine. Have you got any money?

Finally, MICHEL VINAVER (born 1927) is possibly the best known of the post-Brechtians, by virtue of Planchon's production of *Pardessus bord*, for the TNP at the Odéon in 1974. Vinaver was born in Paris and his first play to come to the attention of critics and public was *Les Coréens* (The Koreans) performed at Lyons in 1956. *Pardessus bord* (Above Board) is about the takeover of a medium-sized toilet-paper firm, which controls 12 per cent of the French market and whose business expands regularly at the rate of 5 to 10 per cent a year, by an American giant which promotes soft tissues instead of the cruder traditional product. (In 1966 the French used per inhabitant one eighth of the amount of toilet paper used by the Americans.)

The plot is Brechtian in the manner of the *Rise and Fall of the State of Mahagonny*, or *Arturo Ui*. The old managing director of the French firm dies from a heart attack when the competitive pressures become too fierce; his family continue the fight; a tremendous publicity campaign is mounted to boost the home product. Finally, when the firm has proved its worth and won its fight, its request for more capital is refused by the Bank of Paris and it has to merge anyway with the American giant. It has kept its identity, but win or lose in the competitive market, Vinaver's verdict is that the Americans will get you in the end.

Vinaver has worked in an enterprise such as he presents, but he clearly must have viewed it with all the terror and simplicity of a Catholic virgin forced to inhabit a brothel. It is pathetically unreal, and Planchon used it for a display of technical virility: the biceps of sound and vision are flexed every two or three minutes. It has little of the folk-play humour and trappings with which Brecht enlivened his sermons; it lacks the underlying unconscious sympathy Brecht felt for even his most unsalubrious capitalist villains.

The ability and need to spread such a simple faith and the no less inconsiderable capacity to find listeners only goes to show how far Marxism is usurping the Jesuit tradition in the theatre; but also indeed how Marxism can become as concerned with purity of motives, and as removed from the actual practice of life, as ever Christianity is, or was. Often in such collective enterprises the theatre becomes a temple of utilitarian virtue in which faith is renewed in the company of a like-minded congregation, the affluent hell is castigated, only to be conveniently forgotten the following morning when the bus is boarded, or the car driven off to work. Imaginative hypocrisy is the besetting evil of Marxist theatre.

The importance of café-théâtre has grown considerably in the last six or seven years. In 1966 the official guide, *Pariscope*, did not give it a mention: now, a whole section several pages long is devoted to it. Admission is included in the price of a drink. In one popular café-théâtre, L'Absidiole, lying in the left-bank shadow of Nôtre Dame, there is no back room but, when drinks have been served the bar itself is screened off, a few concealed spotlamps are turned on, and the waiters become the actors. The café-théâtre repertoire is very mixed. The plays themselves last from a quarter to three quarters of an hour; some are influenced, still, by Ionesco and Pinget, as well as by glossy erotic magazines and the films of Jean-Luc Godard. The authors or 'micro-authors' as one of their number has described them, are primarily French (Tardieu, Haïm, Obaldia have all had plays included in one company's programme), but may also include a Mrozek (*At Sea* is a favourite play), a Tennessee Williams, or a von Hofmannsthal. The new work is not of a very high quality, but seems at its best with spectacles influenced by the Theatre of Cruelty (a 'collage' based on de Sade, for example), or surrealist, dadaist experiments in which some short idea or image can be sharply established. There is not the time or space to develop much else. Nevertheless, café-théâtre is a popular marginal theatre, and without receiving any support from the State it has created a faithful and enthusiastic following for itself. The most tenaciously alive include the Café-théâtre des Halles (which began as Le Fanal on the Ile Saint-Louis), which has performed 45 plays in five years, using 115 different actors and 34 directors; and the Sélénite, which presents six short plays in the course of an evening, in two rooms.

The programme at the Sélénite may show a straight Tennessee Williams, as well as something in the *Oh Calcutta* tradition, *Mon cul sur la commode* (Backside on the Commode) described as an 'erotic-hysterical' comedy 'after' Aristophanes. Later on in the evening may be seen, for instance, *Le Dernier Tango dans la jungle* (Last Tango in the Jungle); midnight is the hour for *Charlotte story*, the life of a waitress with 'psycho-erotic' problems. As in London, it appears the critics have now abandoned their early enthusiasm for this form of theatre, leaving it to plough its path as best it can.

II Jean Anouilh

Charlotte: If I take a lover one day, he'll be a left-wing intellectual. Tall and dark and athletic, but not common of course, very well-bred. We'll make love, obviously—you have to when you take a lover—but most of all, we'll talk. We'll talk about everything—at last! It would be marvellous to talk and talk about the Cuban revolution, or the colour problem, lying on a tiger skin, in front of a log fire, drinking whisky . . . after we'd made love. And his voice would be soft and deep, a bit like that young may who played tennis at the Montmachous. Antoine never wants to talk about anything. He says it makes no difference anyway and intellectuals' salvia never modified one single hard fact. What a brute he is!

Les Poissons rouges

Little is known about Jean Anouilh. He has been known to make only one biographical statement, in a letter to H. Gignoux, in 1946:

'I have no biography, and I am very happy with it so. I was born June 23, 1910, at Bordeaux, I came to Paris young, I attended Colbert Pimary School and Chaptal College. A year and a half at the law faculty in Paris, two years in an advertising agency, where I learned to be exact and ingenious, which for me was a substitute for the study of literature. After *L'Hermine* (The Ermine, 1932) I decided to earn my living solely by the theatre, and a little film work. It was folly, but I did well in making that decision. I got by without journalism, and I have on my conscience, in the cinema, one or two comic sketches, and some forgotten and unsigned lyrics. The rest is my life, and . . . I shall keep the details to myself.'

Anouilh is the son of a tailor and a violinist: his mother apparently played in a casino orchestra. In 1931 Louis Jouvet took him on as his secretary, showing no interest in his literary ambitions, and giving him the nickname 'Anouilh le miteux' (Anouilh the shabby). It has been reported that, when his daughter Catherine was born, the playwright was so hard up that she had to sleep in a suitcase. But fortune changed, and a later detail which has escaped is that Anouilh now owns innumerable houses bought with his royalties, in France and elsewhere, and spends much time travelling between them.

In the 1960s he wrote little, a fact which is attributed to the attacks made on him by Paris critics. For someone supposed to epitomize the successful bourgeois dramatist, no one has been more vilified and abused. Even very recently, in London, he showed this power of awakening critical disapproval: one critic wrote of the first British performance of a new play *Tu Etais si gentil quand tu étais petit* (You

Were So Sweet When Little, 1973) that it was 'relentlessly trite' and that the theme, the confrontation of age and youth in the Orestes story, was 'the least palatable aspect of the play'. Another wrote that Anouilh's treatment of Greek myth was redundant.

L'Hermine, to which Anouilh referred as the play which set him off on his career, ran for only 37 performances. His reputation was really established in 1937 with *Le Voyageur sans bagage* (Traveller without Luggage) and was cemented with the historic production of *Antigone* in February 1944. Like Montherlant's *Fils de personne* and *Demain il fera jour*, *Antigone* is an extremely ambiguous work, and earned Anouilh praise for his patriotism and abuse for his treachery depending on whether the audience identified with Antigone or with Créon, though most saw in Antigone's defiant refusal, and her persistent disobedience, the plight of France under the Vichy government.

Antigone is Anouilh's greatest play: it has a resonance, a depth and grandeur which none of his plays since has achieved, and it distils a genuine tragic pathos:

> 'And then [says the Chorus in this play] it's restful, tragedy is, as one knows there's no more hope, no more dirty little hope, that one's caught, that finally one's caught like a rat, with all heaven at one's back, and one can only shout—not groan, oh no, not moan—but scream at the top of one's voice what there is to say, what one's never said and what one never even knew perhaps till then how to say ...'

The personal preoccupation with the *acte gratuit*, as André Gide calls it, of Antigone's determination to bury her brother, may confuse sincerity with truth as some French Catholic critics like H. Gignoux have pointed out, but it mirrors a political reality as few plays have ever been able to. Many critics have seen Créon, who stands for order at the expense of self-expression, as the real hero of the play, and the way Anouilh has dealt with the story makes one never quite sure when, if ever, he is out of sympathy with the middle-aged benign dictator, whose point of view is always sensible and straightforward.

Anouilh can be accused with justification of defending the decay and natural corruption of man: no other modern dramatist is as prepared to give evil such a human face. It is a very Shakespearian quality, and indeed Anouilh once wrote an article humbly entitled 'Devant Shakespeare je me sens encore comme un apprenti étonné' (Before Shakespeare I still feel like an amazed apprentice). Possibly this quality is common to all great theatrical craftsmen, though Sartre has made it clear he despises it: it is certainly a quality he never possessed himself: in a statement directed at Anouilh he said:

> 'The bourgeoisie thinks according to the rules of what I would call a pessimistic naturalism ... that which is human, with the bourgeoisie, is that which is wicked, since they always say "it's human nature".'

Antigone has been nevertheless very highly praised by Sartre, and it possesses, together with Sartre's *Huis clos* and Camus' *Le Malentendu* (*The Misunderstood*, 1944), the striking features of a popular form which is both intellectual and almost violently passionate. The boulevard theatre of the Sacha Guitry variety was far from dead during the Second World War, and it is remarkable how a number of great dramatists were able to fuse popular and sophisticated styles in a way which has never been achieved since in France.

In 1944 audiences were perhaps more disposed to give attention to weighty themes: Claudel's *Le Soulier de satin* held them spellbound night after night for five hours: even Beckett's *Waiting for Godot*, not written until much later, owes much to that climate of seriousness and popularity.

In 1946, after *Antigone*, the critic H. Gignoux judged that Anouilh had exhausted his subject and was now 'au pied d'un mur, au fond d'une impasse'. Anouilh himself declared after a burst of productive activity which had included *Le Rendez-vous de Senlis* (1941), *Roméo et Jeannette* (1946), and an optimistic version, if such is possible, of *Médée* (1946), that he would 'abandon his characters a while to their own games' and search 'another path' for his theatre.

Up till then Anouilh had divided his plays into *pièces roses* and *pièces noirs* (broadly, optimistic and pessimistic plays, a distinction believed to be modelled on Shaw's Plays Pleasant and Unpleasant); after the break came a new burst of activity, dividing into *farces* and *pièces brillantes*. *L'Invitation au château* (Ring Round the Moon, 1947) is a perfectly faceted jewel of theatricality, innocent of the painful concerns of *Antigone*. 'Of all the playwrights of modern France . . . Jean Anouilh possesses the most sure sense of the stage,' Harold Hobson has written, and *L'Invitation au château* shows this sense exercised with a spirited gaiety whose intention is solely to entertain. It overwhelmingly gives the lie to critics such as Serge Radine, who in his *Anouilh, Lenormand, Salacrou* accused Anouilh of a profane despair. *L'Invitation* is easily as suitable for revival today as *La Valse des toréadors*, which has recently been successfully revived in New York, unsuccessfully in London.

Peter Brook, *L'Invitation's* first director in London, asked Christopher Fry to adapt it and the version Fry made is a model of exquisite and timeless prose. Brook has described the love intrigue of Hugo, his brother Frédéric, and the confrontations of rich and poor as 'recorded impressions':

'Unlike so many present-day playwrights [it must be remembered Brook was writing in 1950] who are the descendants of a literary school, and whose plays are animated novels Anouilh is in the tradition of the *commedia dell'arte*. Like Chopin, he preconceives the accidental and calls it an impromptu. He is a poet, but not a poet of words: he is a poet of words-acted, of scenes-set, of players-performing.'

Anouilh's brand of perfectionism could not be better defined. Critics have seen from *L'Invitation* onwards, in the plays directly following, *Ardèle ou la marguerite* (1948), a satire on love, in which among various lovers the only pair who are true, both hunchbacks, commit suicide, *Médée* (1948), *La Répétition ou l'amour puni* (1950), and *Colombe* (1951), a decline in Anouilh's sympathy for his heroes, or heroines, and a corresponding growth of affection for corruption and decay, though not many of these critics would go so far as to agree with Sartre that this is because Anouilh is essentially a reflector of bourgeois values. Many critics whom Sartre would call bourgeois find Anouilh decadent and disgusting, especially in *Colombe*, in which he sends up the theatrical profession: one is J.-J. Gautier of *Le Figaro* who, after stating at length how everyone would be prudishly enraged at Anouilh's bad language and sauciness, and ought not to be, went on to say:

> 'on the other hand, the critics, men of letters, and theatre people in general were very few in deploring that Jean Anouilh, whose life is the theatre, to which he owes his fame, to which he owes everything, all that he's been, all he is, and all he ever will be, tears theatre people limb from limb in play after play, always with greater bitterness and greater savagery. He ridicules them, reviles them, besmears them as if he delighted in it. It must give him some gruesome pleasure to show how ugly and how atrocious they are. Why, Jean Anouilh, why?'

One of the answers to M. Gautier's question appears to be that Anouilh has adopted, since the war, a comic and peripheral approach to the central problem of any one play. Tragic identification, such as one is able to practise in *Antigone*, is sidestepped, and the structure, while still retaining its impeccable sense of form, moves more towards episodic comedy, such as Molière used in *Dom Juan* or *Les Fourberies de Scapin*, and further away from the concentration of tragedy or the equations of the problem play. In the early tragedy, it appears, Anouilh could indulge his sense of innocence, and his rebellious figures who stand out for truth or freedom; in the dark comedy into which Anouilh's work has now resolved, he can indulge his bitter sense of tragic inadequacy at the expense of the figures he mocks. Indeed one could well claim, on the basis of the comedies produced in the early 1970s, *Cher Antoine ou l'amour raté* (Failed Love, 1969), or *Les Poissons rouges ou mon père, ce héro* (The Goldfish, or That Hero My Father, 1970), both written round the figure of the playwright Antoine de St Fleur, that Anouilh's comic vision of despair is now much more genuinely and consciously expressing a sense of absurdity than anything in the French theatre since Camus' *Caligula*. Antoine's defence of the indissolubility of marriage as the 'one guarantee one has of not making a fool of one-self twice over' smacks decidedly of absurdist philosophy.

Anouilh's remaining plays since *Colombe* are *La Valse des toréadors* (Waltz of the Toreadors, 1952), *Cécile ou l'Ecole des pères*, (Cecile or the School for Fathers, 1952), *Jézabel* (1952, though written much earlier), *L'Alouette* (The Lark, 1953), *Ornifle ou le Courant d'air* (1955), *Pauvre Bitos ou le Dîner de têtes* (Poor Bitos, 1956), *L'Hurluberlu ou le Réactionnaire amoureux* (The Fighting Cock, 1959), *Becket ou l'Honneur de Dieu* (1959), *La Grotte* (The Cavern, 1961), *La Foire d'empoigne* (The Fair Seized, 1962) *Le Boulanger, la boulangère et le petit mitron* (The Baker, His Wife, and His Little Assistant, 1969), *Cher Antoine, Les Poissons rouges, Ne réveillez-pas madame* (1970), and *L'Arrêt* (The Arrest).

In all these the familiar Anouilh themes occur and recur: cynicism versus innocence, principle versus selfishness, love versus decay, and so on. But with the exceptions of *L'Alouette* and *Becket*, which are objective (Anouilh uses Augustin Thierry's account of the conquest of England by the Normans as his historical source), the issues are never so clear-cut, but have become as many-sided and devious as life itself.

These exceptions—*L'Alouette* and *Becket*—still do not possess the direct passion of *Antigone*. Although *Antigone* is presented as a tragedy that has already taken place and one knows its direct consequences—as if the attitudes of inevitability Sophocles gives to the chorus have been put by Anouilh into the mouths of the main characters—there is still a powerful dialectic in the form itself. The narrative of *Becket* or of *L'Alouette* is presented at one further remove from reality than in *Antigone*: the ultimately happy outcome of both of the former is known from the start. The splendid opening of *Becket* presents straight away the image of the penitent king, 'nu sous un vaste manteau', who throws off the cloak and falls on his knees in front of his victim's tomb. 'Well, Thomas Becket,' he says:

'Are you satisfied? I am naked at your tomb and your monks are coming to flog me. What an end to our story! You, rotting in this tomb, larded with my barons' dagger thrusts, and I, naked, shivering in the draught, and waiting like an idiot for those brutes to come and thrash me.'

The action is then shuttled back and forth with energy and skill, the history domesticated, made vivid with an earthy flavour. But the audience's identification with Becket and the king although encouraged intellectually is never very deep: there is nothing alarming and sublime in Becket's murder, in the way that T. S. Eliot's *Murder in the Cathedral* attains an overpowering emotion of joy and martyrdom, as well as a genuinely cathartic comedy, when the slayers offer their justifications. Anouilh's method is abrupt, episodic, yet there is a winning simplicity in the portrayal of Becket himself.

Whether Anouilh is, as Irving Wardle wrote in *The Times* when *Cher Antoine* was performed at Chichester, 'all circumference and no centre', or whether as Harold Hobson, his most passionate advocate, has written 'he exemplifies that very skill as a conjurer which highminded, ponderous people sometimes humourlessly take as proof that he is not a major dramatist at all', there is little doubt that Anouilh's skill is as fresh and vivid today as it was in the middle and late thirties. Of his most recent plays, *Les Poissons rouges ou mon père, ce héro* lacks the theatricality and lightness of touch of *Cher Antoine* but more than compensates for this absence in the way Antoine voices his thoughts with the comic reactionary fervour of an Alceste; indeed Jean Dutourd, writing of the 1970 Paris production in *France-Soir* remarked 'I felt a breath of Molière in it ... how refreshing this man is for whom the poor, the moth-eaten, the revolutionary, the demanding, the obscure, the downtrodden, is not sacred.' Yet although there is a distinctively autobiographical ring in the denunciations—Antoine is shown as an enemy of universal suffrage and unemployment pay, regretting the increasing pressure put upon people in society to behave in a collective manner, and he begs for people to be left to be unhappy and clumsy on their own—there is also a lightness of touch which often lifts the play into high comedy. The brilliant opening, for example, when Antoine is caught urinating into the goldfish bowl by his grandmother, can have few precedents as *coup de théâtre*; the bicycle rides and war flashbacks of Antoine and La Surette, and Antoine's black trial for sincerity of intentions, are comedy of the highest order, but dark comedy, the comedy of Molière's *Tartuffe* or *Le Bourgeois gentilhomme*. Anouilh appears to be getting a great deal off his chest in *Les Poissons rouges*, as if for too long he has resented not being taken seriously. The doctor says, for instance, that controversy is a basic essential in a democratic society, and Antoine replies 'Not to me it isn't.'

> 'That's why I never argue, either about politics, or about love. Those are subjects people have kept quiet about for centuries, and it's only since everybody meddles in them that nothing works any more. There was a time when politics was the business of politicians and love the business of whores. *They* were the marriage counsellors and, let me tell you, they knew a bit more than yours do! Today, everybody wants to be a politician, and everybody wants to be a whore.'

Or, in the famous passage to which Jean Dutourd referred when Antoine gives a sudden furious shout, there is a distinct and poignant autobiographical note.

> 'Couldn't people be left alone to be clumsy and miserable in peace the way they've always been? And to grope their way, as they've always done, more or less happily, towards earning their living, their liberty and their love, in their own way. . . . He's shrivelling to death from social security, is your Man. He daren't even fart without making sure he can claim compensation for it!'

One might claim that the speaker is Anouilh the old man turning in anger, but any superficial comparison one might make with John Osborne is immediately dispelled when the doctor departs from Antoine and the actress, Antoine's mistress, who has taken an overdose, wakes up: one is jerked straight back into the basic situation of a classic French comedy. The autobiographical outpouring is strictly contained and never becomes an end in itself.

In the same year as *Les Poissons rouges, Ne réveillez-pas madame* was also highly successful, bringing Anouilh yet another long run at the Comédie des Champs-Elysées. No recent play demonstrates better Anouilh's ability to dominate the théâtre de boulevard. The hero this time is not a playwright but a theatre director, Julien Paluche. He was born in 1914, and his father escaped gloriously from Verdun only to die a few months later from diabetes. His mother, an actress, was already in the toils of her profession, and was notoriously unfaithful to him. Little Julien, replacing his sailor-hat with her lover's topper on temporary loan, receives an early flavour of the salacious boards when he witnesses his concupiscent mother at 'rehearsals'. This spurs him on: he too ploughs through two marriages of his own, trying to fix up his own children with a meal or two to keep them going while forging on towards his opening nights. His interior life is probed, through flashback technique which Anouilh employed notably in *Pauvre Bitos*, and snatches of his past life find analogies in the present.

Ne réveillez-pas madame again abounds with unexpected and superb theatrical sleights of hand. The little boy dancing about in the top hat, the Louis XIV setting painted on a backcloth, which is inexplicably lowered and raised during the announcement of the death of Paluche's mother, serve most forcibly to show that Anouilh has achieved a nonchalance of expertise few can rival. Sartre has written 'in the theatre the intentions [of the playwright] don't count. What counts is what comes out.' By Sartre's own criterion, Anouilh's triumph has been thorough, well sustained and extremely well deserved.

12 Directors

In the wings: medium shot of the Director, overjoyed, and the three Authors, tight-lipped and bilious.
Director (exuberant): Ah! A triumph! ... A triumph! Unforgettable.
Authors (in chorus): An unprecedented shame!
Les Enfants du paradis, 1943.

As in England, the director has come to occupy an increasingly central role in the French theatre. A group of directors and actors known as 'le Cartel des Quatre' was formed in 1926. The 'Cartel' consisted of Charles Dullin, Louis Jouvet, Georges Pitoëff, and Gaston Baty; it had no other policy than a rejection of cruder forms of Zolaesque naturalism, and a united dislike of commercial values. Nevertheless, since its inception, the profession of director has become crucial to the production of any play as, at the very least, a kind of minimum insurance that an effort would be made towards transforming the words and ideas of a given text into the specific language of the theatre, into gesture, involvement, colour, form. The Cartel's influence was primarily on the presentation of the written text. No account of it could improve on that of Barrault, in his memoirs:

'In France the apostles were four, Louis Jouvet, the "Engineer" —from Sabattini's machinery to the smallest recesses of Molière, he knew every bolt, ball bearing, sailor's knot and mercury lamp. The mechanics of the stage never caught him out. He belonged to the seventeenth century.

'Gaston Baty was the "Ensemble Man". The stage of the Théâtre Montparnasse, all clothed in black, resembled the bellows of the plate cameras you see in old prints. Baty used to wear a wide-brimmed hat and loosely knotted cravat. When he pressed the bulb of the camera, he produced miracles worthy of Méliès or Nadar. His theatre was the only one where scene changes made no noise. He might have lived in Flaubert's time.

'Pitoëff took for his own the poetry of the itinerant theatre. Pierrot Lunaire, or Hamlet's John o' Dreams. He seemed to have abolished weight. Through all his travels, he swarmed with children and dreams. Even his accent was winged: in fact, an Elizabethan strolling player. At his start, like all the others, he had been opposed by Antoine, the high priest of the "slice of life". One evening Antoine, beside himself with irritation, had asked him: "Where have you ever seen a room that has no ceiling?" "But . . . in the theatre, monsieur", he had replied.

'Finally, there was Charles Dullin. I shall call him the

"Gardener". He was redolent of the dyed-in-the wool mountebank of every day and age.

'That movement in the theatre—the Cartel, the fruit of Jacques Copeau's Vieux Colombier movement—was based on essential poetry. He had restored to the theatre its honourable place in the fellowship of the Arts. He had joined Dream to Reality again. He was at one and the same time avant-garde and traditional, western and universal. In his fight against the "hands in the pockets" theatre of the Boulevard, he had rediscovered the ramifications that bound it to the great traditions: to the theatre of antiquity, to the *commedia dell'arte*, to the great Spanish and Elizabethan moments, to the Mystery Plays of the Middle Ages and also to the exemplary theatre of the Far East.

'Thrown (by my feeling for caricature, which is indeed a noble art) into a different walk of life, Copeau—"Le Patron"—would have done very well at the Vatican as a cardinal, with a slight Renaissance period tinge; Jouvet, transferred to NASA, would have made modifications in an Apollo rocket; Baty, with a certain mysterious gentleness, would have been an initiate of some secret society; and Pitoëff would be perfect, swinging in the sky of a picture by Chagall.

'As for Charles Dullin, I see him as half-cowboy, half-gangster. The one who, all through the film, seems to be the villain and, at the dénouement, reveals his great heart.'

Artaud's influence on the French directors of today is no less profound; for him the text was secondary to the effect of the whole. A recent example of this influence is Henri Michaux's *Le Drame des constructeurs* (Constructors' Drama, 1930) revived in 1968. This is a short and intense parable to show how the imaginative life of man is imprisoned by authority; the action takes place in a lunatic asylum, but it is not so much a clinical study as a 'prétexte littéraire' for a theme to be explored. Each of the inmates attempts to build a dream, to involve the others in it hopelessly, for he then has his construction brought to a halt by the recurring call to order from the hospital authorities. The loose associative structure, the unreal atmosphere, again anticipate much of the absurd drama that was to follow twenty or thirty years later; the repeated bell to bring the five characters back to their senses is very similar to repetitions of effect in Ionesco, almost identical to the bell in Jack Gelber's *Sleep* which tests a voluntary human guinea-pig's sleep responses. When *Le Drame des constructeurs* was revived the intention was, according to the director, to shock the spectator nervously for thirty-five minutes 'by an alternation of interior dialogue (consisting of silences), and outbursts of sound (voices and electric sound effects)'.

In this, as in other productions where Artaud's influence is strong, the effect of the whole image of a performance dwarfs any human consideration or character, so that the spectator's usual notion of life is upset. The most extreme example of this is a happening described by Sartre in *Un Théâtre de situations* in which a completely nude girl is covered all over in whipped cream which the audience are expected to lick off. Forbidden by the authorities, it conformed to Artaud's dictum that theatre should reveal, by a kind of 'magic operation', the 'libido, violence and sexual obsession' at the heart of everyone.

Jacques Copeau's (1879–1949) attitude to the text used to be reverential: other directors who followed in this tradition, such as Michel Saint-Denis (1897–1968), were altogether self-effacing in their work: any element which called attention to the production was thought to be an intrusion. Jean Vilar, orientated more towards a popular left-wing theatre, believed the director must be 'assassinated' in order that the actor should gain freedom to explore his part, while Roger Planchon set himself, to begin with, simply the task of imitating Brecht.

ANTOINE BOURSEILLER (born 1930) cultivates a certain baroque extravagance, both in what he chooses to direct (he is responsible for the running of the Centre Dramatique of the South West, based on Aix-en-Provence and Marseilles) and the means he uses. Primarily he is an eclectic who leans quite heavily on both surrealist and expressionistic traditions. He is concerned with novelty of effect and also orientated towards visual shock, and he has been criticized for the highly cerebral designs he sometimes imposes on his work. His view is that any production must 'find' itself, establish its own terms on which to live.

His production of *Dom Juan* at the Comèdie-Française, which for the first time took with a Molière classic the kind of liberties now commonplace with Shakespeare, had a *succès de scandale* when it opened. Even the Prime Minister was called upon to give his view, and M. Pompidou, then Prime Minister, professed himself pleased, in spite of 'certains excès'. *Dom Juan* is one of Molière's dark plays and Molière's hero, far from being the disarming degenerate of legend, is a cold miscreant whose pride is directed towards destroying the fundamental beliefs of his society—those of marriage, religion, family, and honour. Narrative is nearly absent, substituted by icy tableaux which contain some of Molière's finest formal speeches, stretched together in a thin tight-rope of continuity.

Bourseiller's approach was to make *Dom Juan* modern; he claimed, in a television interview, an enormous range of modern equivalents—the man returned home after being in a concentration camp, the man faced with Vietnam. Yet it was evident he was after something much more shocking by the way he affronts the normal audience's staid expectations at the Comèdie-Française, in his use of disturbing and baroque visual forms in the sets and costume. He succeeded in achieving this, but with a certain sacrifice of consistency. He is more effective when he directs a modern play, like Philippe Adrien's *La Baye*; here the style called for is both earthy and formal, and Bourseiller's capacity both to surprise and shock is turned to excellent comic effect.

JEAN-LOUIS BARRAULT (born 1910) transforms producing a play into an 'act of love', into 'spiritual coïtus', for the audience to achieve 'orgasm' (these are images Barrault himself uses constantly). His early work, primarily as an actor, was largely concerned with mime and stylized gesture. When he started directing at the Comèdie-Française in 1943 during the Occupation, he turned to conventional plays: *Phèdre, Soulier de satin, Antony and Cleopatra*. When he and his wife Madeleine Renaud left the Comédie-Française to run the Marigny, his repertoire of plays then demonstrated an immense catholicity of choice and range of gifts—Anouilh, Beckett, Ionesco, Billetdoux, Claudel, Genet. The Compagnie Barrault-Renaud, with or without a permanent home, has been virtually the most famous and successful company in France for thirty years, and is still, with their new theatre. Barrault was dismissed from his most recent national post, that of director of the Théâtre de l'Odéon, in 1968, when the theatre was seized by insurgent students. The post was conferred on him, and then taken away from him, by André Malraux who, ironically, was far more left-wing in his youth than Barrault was or ever will be. Barrault is not in the slightest interested in politics: but he is a champion of vitality.

Since 1968 Barrault has returned more to the style of his early years, with his enthusiasm for surrealism and his love of the magic appeal of Artaud finding expression in *Rabelais* and *Jarry sur la butte*, among other works in his prolific output. His company was established for a while in the elegant Théâtre Récamier, but has now occupied the hitherto deserted Gare d'Orsay, (Orson Welles shot there much of his famous film of Kafka's *Trial* which, in a dramatized version, was also one of Barrault's great successes.) Barrault has not received a *sou* of subsidy, and has sunk all his own money into the project.

Barrault considered *Rabelais* 'a dramatic game for actors and the audience', and though he wanted an appearance of improvisation and confusion, he insisted, typically, on the necessity for 'style and precision'. It was first performed in the Elysée Montmartre, which in former days was a boxing-ring, and subsequently staged in London by Barrault at the Roundhouse, which used to be a locomotive shed. Of the original production the critic of *Le Monde*, B. Poirot-Delpech, who could always be relied upon for a careful and discriminating response even if, as on this occasion, he was carried off into uncharacteristic rhetoric, wrote 'that Barrault is alive is confirmed in his dozens of roles, his eclectic choice of repertory, his brave power of bringing life to art, and his extraordinary mystique of germinating abundance'.

Poirot-Delpech recalled Barrault's appearance as the shipwrecked Jesuit in Claudel's *Le Soulier de satin* twenty-five years before:

'From the moment the castaway from the Odéon reappeared in the Montmartre ring, which served him as a raft, it is this vision of his beginnings in Claudel which is reawoken, as a symbol of his coherence and of his stubborn power of survival. Another sign of headstrong constancy is the way the former pupils of Decroux, in shirt-sleeves, without a trace of rancour or fatigue, works himself to the marrow transforming his three-masted raft in mime—with the same invincible smile from the days of *Les Enfants du paradis* in which Baptiste imitated happiness in order to keep believing in it.

'What a lesson of youth from one approaching sixty! The thick curly hair is still that of the bizarre motorbike killer in *Drôle de drame*; the neck retains the same distinctive tenacity as that of

Corvine making his first entrance in Dullin's *Volpone*; the birdlike eyes never stop gazing on all injustice with the bewilderment of Kafka's Joseph K. . . .'

Poirot-Delpech's image of Barrault is sustained by the Jarry spectacle, in 1970, when Jarry's own apocalyptic creations—Père Ubu, the Pataphysician Dr Faustroll—tilt their lances at bourgeois progress and defy death. In Barrault's adaptation, Jarry's last word, when confronted by a skull and cross-bones, is to ask for a toothpick. The gesture is one with which Barrault is completely in sympathy.

Two of the most distinguished directors of the avant-garde are Roger Blin and Jean-Marie Serreau (who died recently). They possess the finest qualities of directorial skill. Their work is utterly dispassionate, personally disinterested, and faithful to the authors they serve. They serve truth rather than effect.

ROGER BLIN (born 1907) was responsible for the important first productions of Samuel Beckett's plays, *Waiting for Godot*, *Endgame*, *Krapp's Last Tape*, and *Happy Days*, in the first two of which he took part as an actor. But he was also one of the first to put on Adamov's plays, while his most visually impressive achievements have been with Genet's work, especially with *Les Nègres* in 1959, and *Les Paravents* in 1966. Indeed it is quite remarkable how one man who has probably had more influence than anyone else on the significant movements of the French theatre should have been given so little recognition, or discussed so lightly and dismissively. Martin Esslin, for example, mentions him several times in *The Theatre of the Absurd*, but only in passing. Blin is so dedicatedly self-effacing that he gives a critic little to discuss. He possesses qualities which are all too rarely found among the self-promotional hierarchies of theatrical endeavour. Recognition of his unique contribution will come in time, when some of the more ephemeral and spectacular work of his contemporaries will have been forgotten.

Blin clearly possesses extraordinary tact, patience, and tenacity. He was an early disciple of Artaud, and in Baratier's *Désordre a vingt ans* there is a moving sequence in which he describes Artaud declaiming his revolutionary texts to an audience at the Vieux-Colombier which included Camus, Sartre, and Cocteau. But he is a receiver of advice, rather than a proclaimer of precepts, as is witnessed by the collections of letters to him which have been published without his own replies. In one such collection, Genet writes to him concerning the famous Odéon production of *The Screens* 'that you have understood the play as I desired is not surprising, for you are quick to understand and discriminating, but you have had the talent and tenacity to apply your understanding. I would have liked to dissociate myself from this performance: I no longer have the strength to do so. Your spiderlike patience and the degree to which you have succeeded have ensnared me in your web.' There could be no greater tribute to a director than such a one from his author.

JEAN-MARIE SERREAU (1915–73) has also fulfilled the function, though to a much less crucial degree, of gifted midwife to new playwrights, not only, like Blin, with Adamov, but also with

Ionesco's *Amédée* (1954), and *La Soif et la faim* (Hunger and Thirst, 1966), and playwrights foreign to France (he directed Brecht's *Exception and the Rule* in 1949 and Max Frisch's *The Fire-Raisers*). Recently, before his death in 1973, Serreau had turned to ardent advocacy of third-world playwrights such as Aimé Césaire and Keteb Yacine, who have been discussed in an earlier chapter.

Sartre claimed that in the nineteenth century the working class and their families found the centre of Paris too expensive to live in, and were forced out to the suburbs. Hence they stopped going to the theatre, with the result that audiences became exclusively bourgeois and plays lost their wide popular appeal for the very first time in history. JEAN VILAR (1912–71), who was responsible for the inception of the Avignon Festival, and who also built up the TNP at the Palais de Chaillot, had a profound sense of the civic importance of the theatre, and wanted it to reflect society: 'Give me a good society' he said in the early years of the TNP, 'and I'll give you a good theatre.' His choice of repertory was inspired throughout: *Murder in the Cathedral* to begin with in 1944, then Brecht (*Mother Courage, The Resistible Rise of Arturo Ui*), Büchner, Gatti, Giraudoux; and to his direction of these works he brought genuinely popular qualities. His distinctive style began at Avignon, where the open-air circumstances were utilized with a simplicity that he was able to capitalize on in the great amphitheatre of Chaillot. He substituted, as he described it, the 'decorative banners and musical appeal of the open air for the gold and lustre of bourgeois theatre'.

As Jacques Copeau had done before him, he concentrated entirely on text and actor so his approach to a play was very much in the form of a refusal—he refused to impose anything of his own on it. His direction also stemmed primarily from his qualities as an actor. In two of his great performances, as the Hitler figure in *Arturo Ui* and as Robespierre in *Danton's Death*, his deep grating delivery of the text was accompanied by extraordinary economy and lucidity. He joined the heroic grand manner of former days with a cool and modern utilitarian approach, both achieved externally by means of technical restraint and control. He became the perfect middle-aged antagonist for Gérard Philipe, whom he directed in *Le Cid* and *Le Prince de Hombourg*.

In all his work there was little scenery, and he used the stage in width rather than in depth. The placing was always careful, the lighting simple and bold. Inner tension, silence, immobility, these were the distinctive features of a Vilar production. Like Roger Blin, though on a different, more epic and solid canvas, he renounced any claim to originality as a director and, like Blin also, he knew and approached the actor from the inside, because he was one himself.

ROGER PLANCHON (born 1931) has also a greater honesty than most directors, and this has led him, in the end, to start writing his own plays instead of dismembering those of others. In an interview with Michael Kustow he stated 'about nine or ten years ago, in my opinion, a certain number of directors had attained a point of perfection in their productions. Strehler, Brook, people like that, were creating impeccable productions, and they felt the need to change things further. Most of these directors said "let's chop up the text, let's write our own texts collectively". .... I'd already done quite enough of that, and decided I should begin humbly with whatever I was capable of writing.'

So he did. Although he now has some six or seven plays to his credit, which have a strong documentary exactness and sense of truth, Planchon has not, in my view, achieved an identity of his own as a playwright. And he has not altogether freed himself from the influence of Brecht. He says himself that, as a director, 'I was the first one who simply wanted to copy Brecht—copy him pure and simple, without any inhibitions', and then as a playwright that 'all the plays I've written have been a long meditation on Brecht's work. I think the two writers in the world who are the closest to Brecht are Peter Weiss and myself. He's taken one side of him, I've taken the other.'

The side he has taken is the later side, the ambiguous period in which directorial preoccupations pinioned down the simple expressive need for boldness and romantic extremity. There is something very measured about Planchon's work: not, of course, the supremely exuberant parody of *The Three Musketeers* which is still, on occasions, the meal-ticket of Planchon's company. The text is the springboard for total means of expression, and although the scheme and ideas are always interesting, there is something grey and inexpressive about Planchon's writing: but then, he did not begin as a poet, like Brecht. What he writes, in fact, are efficient scenarios for his own productions.

The action of *Bleus, blancs, rouges ou les Libertins* (Blue, White, Red or the Libertines), one of his most ambitious plays, which he wrote in 1967, stretches from the eve of the summoning of the Estates by Louis XVI in October 1788, until 18 June 1800, by which time Bonaparte had won the battle of Marengo, and State and Church had patched up their quarrel. Emigrés had begun to dribble back into the mother country, to fit themselves into the new order. The main character, the Marquis d'Arbonne, is forced into marriage by his father, and has made a vow never to sleep with his wife. After various adventures, incuding an attempt to join Royalist forces which reject him because of his libertinage, and a spell as a strolling violinist, d'Arbonne is reconciled with his wife; eventually he decides to return to Paris in the guise of a bourgeois.

Into this main stream are poured minor tributaries: an officer passes through various shades of loyalty—to the nation against the aristocracy, to Robespierre against the Hébertists, finally to the counter-revolution against the rest of the world. A public scribe, a low-key Falstaffian figure who dances on a table in nothing but a tricolour, has bad moments but survives; noblemen try to hide in a madhouse; a bishop's secretary turns revolutionary and finds his ideal betrayed.

With Planchon's reputation for flamboyance and adventure, one would have thought that *Bleus, blancs, et rouges* would contain a great deal of parody: but it remains a peripheral story, a slow-moving *conte* following a group of characters: it serves to demonstrate the changing pattern of people's lives. It smacks, also, of some of the rosy statements of Voltaire. The creaking tumbrils of revolution are in the background, but they are hard to hear. The situation, after the manner of Brecht, determines the characters; little is given them by way of independent will, passion, or depth. But because they are deprived of any Brechtian judgement of themselves or their dilemmas, they emerge on the frivolous side. Others of his works, like *Le Cochon noir* (Black Pig, 1974) are more sombre and restrained.

Planchon has directed well over fifty plays since 1950, most of them either at the Théâtre de la Comédie at Lyons—he was director there from 1952 to 1957—or at Villeurbanne, where he has remained since 1957, refusing all other posts, such as the TNP in Paris. Now the TNP has been moved to Villeurbanne, and he runs it from there. He has absorbed other influences than Brecht, Vilar for one, especially with regard to the organization of the public; also, the Elizabethans and the classic Spaniards play a part in his method. To Piscator he owes the use of the 'calendar'—a strip of material on which is written commentaries and comments to the public; also, the impeccable 'document' programme—full of back-up material, quotations, print illustrations, and passages from the play.

In his production of Pirandello's *Henry IV*, as in *Bleus, blancs, rouges*, he concentrated on the social or political conduct of the characters, not on their psychology. His *Edward II* was not only a protector of the arts, but an innovator who vainly tried to squash the conspiracies of the barons by wooing the people; *George Dandin* was not only a cuckold who reaps the fruit of his bad match, but a rich peasant, cruelly mocked because he was a peasant; the play becomes a sort of moral lesson, what Brecht would have called a 'Lehrstück', on the class struggle, and Robert Hirsch's celebrated performance later at the Comédie-Française owed much to this interpretation. Although they built up similar types of popular audience, Planchon's approach is diametrically opposite to Vilar's. Planchon used to be an amateur 'cinéaste' and the film director is evident in much of his work—plans of state or spectacular views are projected in *Edward II*; *The Three Musketeers* owes much to the early burlesque movies. But the overall impression he conveys is one of a critical and studied poise.

PATRICE CHÉREAU (born 1944) is the most brilliant of younger French directors. He was taken on at Villeurbanne by Planchon, in order that the latter could devote less time to directing and more to writing his own plays. Chéreau's work was first seen at the Paris suburb of Sartrouville where he was running the theatre and presenting an exotic programme (Mayakowsky's *Les Bains, Pièces chinoises, Le Prix de la révolte au marché noir*—the last, one of many plays which conducted a post-mortem on the uprising of May 1968).

The *Pièces chinoises* come from the golden period of Chinese drama after the Mongol invasion; their formality and conventions have a peculiarly modern simplicity (Brecht was very attracted to the same style: on it he based *The Good Woman of Setzuan*). In the first play of Chéreau's called *Snow in the Middle of Summer*, a young lady is shown falsely accused of poisoning her foster-father with a mutton soup, and is set free on the judgement of a spendidly corrupt Azdak figure who clowns with his clerk and prostrates himself for gifts in front of the court. In the second, *The Wife Thief*, an evil and domineering baron goes about the country stealing wives, and passing them on to others when he has had enough of them. In both plays, an all-gracious Emperor restores justice and order, though in the second the lovely series of reconciliations is dramatically shattered by the main character who refuses to go back to his family.

The texts are unnaturalistic and formal, and Chéreau uses a striking invention typical of his method. Doing away with the subtle gesture-language of the past, he turns the stage itself into a giant and versatile machine. It has multiple traps in a steeply raked and planked floor, token décors wound in on wires, indeed a whole visible stage which can be cranked up on ropes, and revolving cylinders which spring props into view. All help to shift the action with stunning rapidity, and with the cast using a style of violent expressiveness and half-comic posturing, the men in masks, one begins to suspect that Chéreau invented the plays for his own manner of staging them.

His highly acclaimed production of Marivaux's *La Dispute* was part of the 1973 Paris festival. Marivaux's original play would hardly last an hour if it were played without interruption, while Chéreau's production lasts over two and a half and is a stunning event with revolutionary lighting effects, as in the *Pièces chinoises*, and a de Sade framework which heightens the surreal possibilities of the plot. The plot itself is built round an experiment conducted by a prince overlording the artificial fostering of four children who are subsequently let loose. Planchon has said of Marivaux that 'there's a peculiarly modern tension between his characters, between their appetites and feelings on the one hand and their social code of behaviour on the other.'

Chéreau exploits Marivaux's ironies literally, for example in the last scene the Prince and his entourage cross on to the stage (having been placed on a rostrum in the stalls) and are trapped with the subject of their experiment. But in this, as in the *Chinese Plays*, and the revolution play, Chéreau shows his capacity for expanding the images conveyed by words or ideas into a visual spectacle of breathtakingly epic proportions and impeccably disciplined taste. The director is always the star of the show.

Another young director who is physically the star of his own show is JÉRÔME SAVARY (born 1945). Unlike Chéreau, he is well known in London on account of his productions of *Robinson Crusoë* and *From Moses to Mao: 5000 Years of Love and Adventure* at the Roundhouse (1972 and 1974). Savary is self-indulgent, shocking and flamboyant, a follower of Artaud lightened with a touch of the old-fashioned Music Hall. For instance, in *Oratorio macabre du radeau de la Méduse* he animates Géricault's famous painting of the effects of a shipwreck, and this results in a grotesque and stunning vision. It is performed by twenty almost nude men, one deep-voiced whore, one beautiful woman, one five-years-old child (Savary's own), and a front row of chorus girls wearing enormous seaweed hats. Savary, who plays drums throughout, conducts the *Oratorio* from the front row of the circle. A net is spread over the stalls to represent the sea, and in it the shipwrecked unfortunates topple or plunge to their deaths within inches of the audience.

Savary's text, as in all his shows, is an uneven collage of wit, anguish, and uninhibited obscenity. The grisly parable is a progress through orgy, the pure essence of loving, to cannibalism and the complete death of hope. The orgy scene itself, mimed with convincing and revolting frankness, is given a contrapuntal effect by the ship's officers' singing hymns. The holocaust is some of the most effective and most spontaneous Theatre of Cruelty one will ever see—the dying exchange cups of urine, and hang up intestines on a string tied to the mast. The horror is purged at the very end by a fine image of redemption on the backcloth—huge white insects with moving wings, while the whore totters towards the mast with her arms spread. In this, as in the later spectacles, Savary is the master of ceremonies, a function he performs with an extraordinary zest and command.

ARIANE MNOUCHKINE (born 1939) first came to notice with her production of Arnold Wesker's *The Kitchen* in the old Montmartre Circus ring. Her large company is mostly an amateur one in origin, consisting of teachers and artisans who are dedicated to the ensemble conditions of work, and since 1970, when they established themselves in an old cartridge factory in Vincennes, they have performed two collective works on the French Revolution, *1789* and *1792*. Each production is the result of detailed and thorough preparation: rehearsals last for several months, and the actors devote their whole life to the company, living together and sharing box office receipts as a co-operative, like the Living Theatre. Their dedication is admirable, and they perform daily improvisations, engage in group research projects, and live and operate together as a team. This cohesion and discipline shows in all their productions.

In terms of public esteem Mnouchkine's company was undoubtedly forged in the heat of Wesker's *Kitchen*, and the unceasing frenetic style they use in *1789* has much in it of the unflagging work routines, the behaviourist zoo, that Wesker created. Clowns, jugglers, mountebanks are at the centre of *1789*, and the whole revolution emerges like a papier mâché mock-up.

In directing *A Midsummer Night's Dream* on a vast expanse of white fur in a circus ring (1967), Mnouchkine fulfilled an early abandoned ambition of Jean Cocteau to play *The Dream* in a circus, and provided encouragement for Peter Brook's refinement of the idea in his own famous and later production. Mnouchkine called *The Dream* 'the most violent and savage play anyone could ever dream', and her production faithfully fulfilled this notion. Puck was cruel, bloodstained, and manic; the two pairs of lovers bled their emotions in a frustrated frenzy that barely touched upon the wit of the original. Titania's train of fairies looked like Red Indian chiefs and Theseus' bodyguard like Assyrians; Theseus had the white-robed air of an Indian prophet. It was a disenchanting view of the play, stripping the pure fairyland of Shakespeare's imagination down to its potential sado-masochism and throwing into relief the transforming power of Mnouchkine's abilities.

Postscript on French acting

'I believe that an art is so much the more rich as it is poor in means.'

Etienne Decroux

A stack of leather-bound books is spotlighted in the centre of a crucifix-shaped stage. An actor in ordinary clothes climbs on to the side of the crucifix and strikes a gong to mark the beginning of the performance. Other actors enter from all four sides of the crucifix, and gather round the pile of books. One strikes a match and burns a book. They begin by saying 'society is a sort of prison full of sinners, in which order has to be maintained by force.'

It could be Sartre . . . Genet; it could be Stendhal; it might even be Samuel Beckett parodying Stendhal, Sartre, or Genet. But by the sixth line, we can detect an element none of these three possesses . . . 'some people have a wonderful gaiety of heart, Born of a contempt for the quirks of Fate. For want of a better name, we call it Joy.' And then the dome of the building seems to disdain all that man is, all mere complexity, as they leap into the famous hymn of physical and verbal exuberance extracted from the works of Rabelais by Jean-Louis Barrault.

The Japanese call actors 'dispensers of oblivion', and this might fairly be described as Barrault's attitude. He uses the actor to bring life to the text but the text is like an element of nature into which the actor pours his means of expression—lyrical diction, breathing, sighing, symbolical and lyrical gestures of the body. Barrault, more than any other figure in the French theatre today, contradicts Chateaubriand's criticism of his time 'we are content with small beauties when we are incapable of large ones.' He attempts to restore acting, defined as 'the art of the human being in space', back to its rightful place, the theatre. It is an an utterly different approach to the theatre from the English one: English theatre has changed profoundly since the 1950s, and not necessarily for the better—as the attraction of the a pre-1950 style of production like Sartre's adaptation of *Kean*, with Alan Badel, demonstrated not long ago. The younger English actor today is analytical, irreverent, unified with his fellow professionals not by a hierarchical respect for great performers or performances, but by a need for explanations. Catechism, and a conviction only grudgingly won, are a substitute for faith. For Barrault the theatre is still believed in—the myth, the rite, above all the physical involvement. 'Stanislavsky's method', he has said, 'is seductive, but a little too illusory. That of Brecht drives home, alas, some truths, but it is not gay.' The text must always be recognized as a text. An English actor like Nicol Williamson will tear himself to

92

pieces in front of an audience: his performance is a well-sustained event: a happening. Barrault in performance is a work of art: he will only *seem* to be tearing himself to pieces. At the surrealist level of nervous excitement, Williamson's performance may be electrifying, but this is at the level of stimulus, not necessarily of excellence (in Williamson's case the two go together). The French actor does not share the Anglo-Saxon need for total exposure; he likes to preserve a sense of mystery.

Barrault is still one of the world's greatest acting mechanisms. He has an acute and sensitive mind. He has the richest physical gifts, a face of astonishing expression, a body which, for its harmony of movement and its quality of relaxation, has never been rivalled. To watch him carry a stick of wood as a heavy burden across the stage is a revelation: to watch his physique registering torment through those great sets of muscles that line his neck and chest, and then, with a sudden flick, see him relax, shake himself free, is a rich and crowning experience; or that smile which one moment is full of life, or the eyes that can be completely dead, the brow completely ravaged.

The body is Barrault's emotional centre: movement and expression provide a geography of emotions. Otherwise, there is no engaged and hurtful conflict in what his mind sees, and in what his body can express.

His wife, Madeleine Renaud, has that centre in her very being. In every performance she gives, her joy and charm, her sadness, her despair, are utterly unfeigned and natural, and the feeling she conveys, even sometimes highly sentimental feeling (as in *Harold et Maude*, with which they opened the Théâtre d'Orsay in 1974), is illuminated by grace and pure technique. There is something trance-like about the greatness of her acting, something closely akin to religious experience. One appreciates its artificiality, as when she might stare at one moment at a dead piece of painted canvas on the stage, face lighting up with the joy of unlimited freedom: one knows nothing is there, yet she has the capacity of making one only too eager to participate in the illusion.

But if Renaud's expression of joy can approach religious ecstasy, she can also fill her parts with flesh and blood. She can make one feel the sadness of passing time with an extraordinary poignance, as she did in Samuel Beckett's *Oh les beaux jours*!

She peels away all extraneous emotion, and this can make the simplicity all the more telling in its contrast to the excessive demonstrations of the parts of others. Above all, as she has demonstrated so amply, she has the capacity to achieve final and memorable climaxes. In *Harold et Maude*, Maude takes her own life on her eightieth birthday. How she does this is not specified: dressed in white, Renaud shows her die. She transfixes herself into an utter stillness, as if, by some sleight of hand, she has passed on her spirit while leaving her body behind, visibly breathing, on the stage.

Barrault and Renaud are still at the peak of their fame and influence, but they are the last of a generation, many of whom are no longer alive. There is still, of course, Edwige Feuillère, not only famous for her interpretation of *La Dame aux camélias*, but strikingly successful in the *Folle de Chaillot* at the TNP in 1965; more recently she has played Agnes in Barrault's over-sentimental production of Albee's *A Delicate Balance*. There is Marie Bell, who created the role of Madame Irma in Peter Brook's production of *Le Balcon*, and who is noted for being an actress-manageress in the nineteenth-century style. But Pierre Brasseur, that extraordinary tornado of physical and emotional energy, is gone. So is Jean Vilar, so indeed is Gérard Philipe, who died before reaching the age of forty, but whose theatrical legend is secure.

There are not many new names that can be associated with the young companies or the new authors, as the governing spirit of this work is directed against the position held by the star, and towards the ensemble. Jean Bouise is an outstanding member of Planchon's troupe, and he has played Brecht's *Schweik* and *La Vie imaginaire de l'éboueur Auguste Geai* (The Imaginary Life of the Garbage Collector Auguste G., 1962) by Armand Gatti; Marie Dubois, Jean-Pierre Cassel, have also done outstanding work in his company.

At the other end of the scale, the Comédie-Française calls upon the services of such stars as Georges Descrières, and the indomitable Robert Hirsch, who has shown, as George Dandin, that he has extraordinary tragic depth as well as comic range. Suzanne Flon remains the outstanding comic actress of her generation, while, among many others, François Périer, Delphine Seyrig, Eléonore Hirt, and the comic actor Rufus have retained their power and their allure.

As Barrault's remark about Brecht and Stanislavsky, quoted above, shows only too well, the French actor is caught between the naturalism of Stanislavsky and the realism of Brecht, without the in-stinctive feeling for them which really does justice to either. The in-stinctive disposition of French acting on the one hand is towards mime as exemplified in the Decroux tradition and practised today by oustanding teachers such as Jacques Lecoq. Lecoq lays the emphasis on a purity of approach, a stripping away of inessentials: 'it is necessary to express oneself in silence, without technique being out-side feeling, in order to give the illusion of life in the solitude of the body, without the mime-actor ever becoming merely a demonstrator, or a virtuoso, or a puppet.'

On the other hand the French actor's instincts propel him towards an almost Jansenist approach to the authority of the text, as exemplified by Copeau and his work at the Vieux-Colombier, which spread into the English theatre through the Old Vic School. At the time of writing this book the desire for 'total theatre', 'Theatre of Cruelty', all forms of expressionism, noise, brutality, shock, con-structivism, as well as mechanical virtuosity—and virtually anonymous performance—has blotted out the ascetic ideal of Copeau. But the ideal itself is not dead. In 1913 Copeau wrote—and it can equally well stand for today:

'A mad industrialism which from day to day more cynically degrades our French stage and repels from it the cultured public; the monopoly of the greater part of a theatre by a handful of enter-tainers in the hire of shameless merchants; everywhere, even in high places, whose authority should bring with it a certain sense of pride, the same spirit of show and speculation, the same lack of taste everywhere; everywhere the spectacle of an art that is dying, and of which there may even be no question any longer, in the parasitic toils of bluff, of auction methods, of exhibitionism; everywhere shallowness, disorder, indiscipline, ignorance and folly; contempt for the artist, hatred of beauty; an overproduction becoming ever more foolish and more futile, a body of criticism becoming ever more complacent, a public taste wandering farther and farther astray: these are what anger us and now drive us to revolt.'

Chart of important productions 1940-75

Year	Event	Title	Author
1940	CHARLES DULLIN leaves l'Atelier JACQUES COPEAU moves to Comédie-Française	*Les Monstres sacrés*	Jean Cocteau
1941	JOUVET in Latin America DULLIN at the Sarah-Bernhardt J-L VAUDOYER at Comédie-Française	*Le Rendez-vous de Senlis* *La Machine à écrire* *Le Bout de la route* *Léocadia*	Jean Anouilh Jean Cocteau Jean Giono Jean Anouilh
1942	GASTON BATY leaves the Théâtre Montparnasse	*Deirdre of the Sorrows* *La Reine morte* *Les Mouches*	J. M. Synge Montherlant J.-P. Sartre
1943		*Sodome et Gomorrhe* *Le Soulier de satin* *Storm* *Le Voyage de Thésée* *Fils de personne* *Am-stram-gram* *Les J3* *Renaud et Armide*	Jean Giraudoux Paul Claudel Strindberg Georges Neveux Montherlant André Roussin Roger-Ferdinand
1944	Death of JEAN GIRAUDOUX	*Antigone* *Huis clos* *Le Malentendu* *Le Bourgeois gentilhomme* *Les Fiancés du Havre*	Jean Anouilh J.-P. Sartre Albert Camus Molière Armand Salacrou
1945	Return of JOUVET	*Murder in the Cathedral* *La Folle de Chaillot* *Caligula* *The House of Bernarda Alba* *Les Bouches Inutiles* *Les Mal aimés*	T. S. Eliot Jean Giraudoux Albert Camus F. García Lorca S. de Beauvoir Mauriac
1946	The Renaud-Barrault Company at Marigny First Competition of Young Companies Death of RAIMU	*Maria* *Of Mice and Men* *Le Père humilié* *Hamlet* *Le Soldat et la sorcière* *Les Incendiaires* *Quoat-Quoat* *Les Nuits de la colère* *Morts sans sépulture* *La P . . . respectueuse* *L'Aigle à deux têtes*	André Obey Steinbeck Paul Claudel Shakespeare Armand Salacrou M. Clavel Audiberti Armand Salacrou J.-P. Sartre J.-P. Sartre Jean Cocteau
1947	First festival held at Avignon	*The Trial* *Les Bonnes* *Dom Juan* *L'Invitation au château* *Mourning Becomes Electra* *La Petite hutte* *L'Archipel Lenoir* *Les Epiphanies* *Passage du matin*	Kafka, Gide Jean Genet Molière Jean Anouilh O'Neill André Roussin Armand Salacrou Henri Pichette Mauriac

Theatre	Production	Cast
Michodière		
Atelier	André Barsacq	
Hébertot		
Noctambules		Alain Cuny
Michodière	Pierre Fresnay	Yvonne Printemps
Mathurins	Marcel Herrand	
Comédie-Française		Maria Casarès
Sarah-Bernhardt	Charles Dullin	Jean Yonnel
Hébertot	Douking	
Comédie-Française	J.-L. Barrault	Edwige Feuillère, Gérard Philipe
Poche	Jean Vilar	Marie Bell
Mathurins	Marcel Herrand	
Saint-Georges		
Athénée		
Bouffes-Parisiens		
Comédie-Française		François Périer
Atelier	André Barsacq	Monelle Valentin, Jean Davy
Vieux-Colombier	R. Rouleau	Michel Vitold, Tania Balachova
Mathurins	Marcel Herrand	Maria Casarès
Comédie-Française		Raimu
Comédie-Française		
Vieux-Colombier	Jean Vilar	
Athénée	Louis Jouvet	
Hébértot	Paul Oettly	Marguerite Moreno
Studio des Ch.-Elysées	Maurice Jacquemont	Gérard Philipe
Carrefours		
Comédie-Française	J.-L. Barrault	Madeleine Renaud
Comédie des Ch.-Elysées		
Hébertot		
Théâtre des Ch.-Elysées		
Marigny	J.-L. Barrault	Cie Renaud-Barrault
Sarah Bernhardt	Charles Dullin	
Noctambules		
Gaîté-Montparnasse	A. Reybaz	
Marigny	J.-L. Barrault	Cie Renaud-Barrault
Antoine		
Hébertot		Jean Marais
Marigny	J.-L. Barrault	
Athénée	Louis Jouvet	
Athénée	Louis Jouvet	
Atelier	André Barsacq	
Montparnasse	Gaston Baty	Marguerite Jamois
Nouveautés		
Montparnasse		Charles Dullin
Noctambules		Gérard Philipe, Maria Casarès
Madeleine		

Year	Event	Title	Author
1948		*L'Etat de siège*	Albert Camus
		Lucienne et le boucher	Marcel Aymé
		Le Voleur d'enfants	Supervielle
		Le Maître de Santiago	Montherlant
		Les Mains sales	J.-P. Sartre
		Yerma	F. García Lorca
		Ardèle ou la marguerite	Jean Anouilh
		Partage de midi	Paul Claudel
1949	Death of DULLIN	*Le Pain dur*	Paul Claudel
	Death of COPEAU	*La Fête noire*	Audiberti
		Haute surveillance	Jean Genet
		Les Œufs de l'autruche	André Roussin
		L'Inconnue d'Arras	Armand Salacrou
		La Nuit des hommes	J. Bernard-Luc
1950		*La Cantatrice chauve*	Ionesco
		L'Invasion	A. Adamov
		La Grande et la petite manœuvre	A. Adamov
		Sire Halewyn	M. de Ghelderode
		La Répétition ou l'amour puni	Jean Anouilh
		Clérambard	Marcel Aymé
		Malatesta	Montherlant
		Le Tartuffe	Molière
		Le Don d'Adèle	Barillet-Grédy
1951	JEAN VILAR at the TNP	*La Leçon*	Ionesco
	Death of LOUIS JOUVET	*Monsieur Bob'le*	Schéhadé
	GÉRARD PHILIPE at Avignon	*Le Diable et le Bon Dieu*	J.-P. Sartre
		Colombe	Jean Anouilh
		Bacchus	Jean Cocteau
		L'Héritière	Ducreux-James
		The Prince of Homburg	Kleist
		Mother Courage	Brecht
1952	Death of GASTON BATY	*Les Chaises*	Ionesco
	Death of PIERRE RENOIR	*La Parodie*	A. Adamov
		Capitaine Bada	Jean Vauthier
		La Farce des ténébreux	M. de Ghelderode
		Nuclea	Henri Pichette
		La Tête des autres	Marcel Aymé
		La Valse des toréadors	Jean Anouilh
		Le Profanateur	Th. Maulnier
		Lorenzaccio	Musset
1953	Death of MARCEL HERRAND	*En attendant Godot*	Beckett
		Victimes du devoir	Ionesco
		Tous contre tous	A. Adamov
		Le Professeur Taranne	A. Adamov
		L'Alouette	Jean Anouilh
		Sud	J. Green
		Zamore	Georges Neveux
		Robinson	Supervielle
		Les Aveux les plus doux	G. Arnaud

Theatre	Production	Cast
Marigny	J.-L. Barrault	
Vieux-Colombier	Douking	Alfred Adam
Œuvre		
Hébertot		Henri Rollan
Antoine		André Luguet, François Périer
Studio des Ch.-Elysées	Maurice Jacquemont	
Comédie des Ch.-Elysées		
Marigny	J.-L. Barrault	Edwige Feuillère
Atelier	André Barsacq	
Huchette	G. Vitaly	
Mathurins	Marcel Herrand	
Michodière	Pierre Fresnay	
Comédie-Française	Gaston Baty	
Atelier	André Barsacq	
Noctambules	Nicolas Bataille	
Studio des Champs-Elysées	Jean Vilar	
Noctambules	J.-M. Serreau	
Noctambules	André Reybaz	
Marigny	J.-L. Barrault	Cie Renaud-Barrault
Comédie des Champs-Elysées		
Marigny	J.-L. Barrault	
Athénée	Louis Jouvet	
Wagram		
Poche	Marcel Cuvelier	
Hutchette	G. Vitaly	R.-M. Chauffard
Antoine	Louis Jouvet	P. Brassuer, J. Vilar, Maria Casarès
Atelier	André Barsacq	Yves Robert, Danièle Delorme
Marigny	J.-L. Barrault	Cie Renaud-Barrault
Mathurins	Marcel Herrand	
Avignon	Jean Vilar	Gérard Philipe
TNP	Jean Vilar	Germaine Montero
Lancry	Sylvain Dhomme	Tsilla Chelton
Lancry	Roger Blin	
Poche	André Reybaz	André Reybaz
Grand-Guignol	Georges Vitaly	
TNP	Gérard Philipe	Mobiles by Calder
Atelier	André Barsacq	Yves Robert, R. Souplex
Comédie des Champs-Elysées	Roland Pietri	
Athénée		Tony Taffin
Avignon	Gérard Philipe	Gérard Philipe, Daniel Ivernel (music by M. Jarre)
Babylone	Roger Blin	Jean Martin, Lucien Raimbourg, Pierre Latour
Quartier Latin	Jacques Mauclair	
Babylone	J.-M. Serreau	
Comédie de Lyon	Roger Planchon	
Montparnasse	Jean Anouilh (décor J-D. Malclès)	Suzanne Flon
Athénée	Jean Mercure	Anouk Aimée, Pierre Vaneck
Atelier	André Barsacq	Yves Robert
Œuvre	Jean Le Poulain	Dominique Blanchar
Quartier Latin	Michel de Ré	Michel Piccoli, Roger Hanin

Year	Event	Title	Author
1953 *(contd.)*		*Siegfried*	Jean Giraudoux
		Kean	Dumas, Sartre
		Dom Juan	Molière
		Les Invités du Bon Dieu	Armand Salacrou
		Christophe Colomb	Paul Claudel
		Pour Lucrèce	Jean Giraudoux
		Il Piacere dell'onestà	Pirandello
		La Maison de la nuit	Th. Maulnier
1954	The Berliner Ensemble presents BRECHT's *Mother Courage* at the First Paris Festival	*La Soirée des proverbes*	Schéhadé
		Amédée ou Comment s'en débarrasser	Ionesco
		Les Naturels du Bordelais	Audiberti
		Les Quatre vérités	Marcel Aymé
		L'Ennemi	J. Green
		Le Mari, la femme et la mort	André Roussin
		La Manière forte	Jacques Deval
		Un nommé Judas	C. A. Puget
		Port-Royal	Montherlant
		Yerma	F. García Lorca
		La Condition humaine	Malraux, Maulr
		Les Sorcières de Salem	Arthur Miller, M. Aymé
1955	Death of CLAUDEL	*Le Ping-Pong*	A. Adamov
		Jacques ou la Soumission	Ionesco
		Nekrassov	J.-P. Sartre
		Ornifle	Jean Anouilh
		Les Œufs de l'autruche	André Roussin
		La Ville	Paul Claudel
		Intermezzo	Jean Giraudoux
		Voulez-vous jouer avec moà?	Marcel Achard
		La Famille Arlequin	Cl. Santelli
		L'Amour fou	André Roussin
		A la nuit la nuit	F. Billetdoux
		Oresteia	Aeschylus
		Orvet	Jean Rneoir
		Triomphe de l'amour	Marivaux
1956		*Les Chaises* (revival)	Ionesco
		Le Personnage combattant	Jean Vauthier
		Magie rouge	M. de Ghelderode
		Le Square	Marguerite Du
		Les Oiseaux de lune	Marcel Aymé
		Requiem for a Nun	Faulkner, Cam
		L'Œuf	F. Marceau
		Les Coréens	Michel Vinave
		Irma la douce	A. Breffort
		Les Fourberies de Scapin	Molière
1957		*Fin de partie*	Beckett, Ionesco
		Le Nouveau Locataire	
		Paolo Paoli	A. Adamov

Theatre	Production	Cast
Comédie des Champs-Elysées	Claude Sainval	Raymond Rouleau
Sarah-Bernhardt	Pierre Brasseur	Pierre Brasseur
TNP	Jean Vilar	Jean Vilar, D. Sorano
Saint-Georges	Yves Robert	
Marigny	J.-L. Barrault	Cie Renaud-Barrault
Marigny	J.-L. Barrault	Edwige Feuillère, Madeleine Renaud
Saint-Georges	Jean Mercure	
Hébertot	Michel Vitold	
Petit-Marigny	J.-L. Barrault	Michel Piccoli, Jean Servais
Babylone	J.-M. Serreau	Lucien Raimbourg
La Bruyère	G. Vitaly	R.-M. Chauffard
Atelier	André Barsacq	
Bouffes-Parisiens	Fernand Ledoux	Maria Casarès
Ambassadeurs	L. Ducreux	
Athénée		Robert Lamoureux
Comédie Caumartin	Jean Mercure	Paul Meurisse
Comédie-Française	Jean Meyer	Jean Debucourt
Huchette	Guy Suarès	Domitella Amural, Genu Athanaziou
Hébertot	Marcelle Tassencourt	
Sarah-Bernhardt	Raymond Rouleau	Yves Montand, Simone Signoret
Noctambules	Jacques Mauclair	Jean Martin, R.-M. Chauffard
Huchette	Robert Postec	J.-L. Trintignant
Antoine	Jean Meyer	Michel Vitold, R.-M. Chauffard
Comédie des Champs-Elysées	Jean Anouilh	Pierre Brasseur
Michodière	Pierre Fresnay	
Avignon	Jean Vilar	Maria Casarès, Georges Wilson, Alain Cuny
Marigny	J.-L. Barrault	Simone Valère, Jean Desailly
Théâtre en rond	A. Villiers	Robert Dhéry, Christian Duvaleix, Jacques Duby
Vieux-Colombier	Jacques Fabbri	
Madeleine	A. Roussin	Jacques Dumesnil
Œuvre	The author	
Marigny	Renaud-Barrault	Marguerite Jamois
Renaissance	Jean Renoir	Leslie Caron
TNP	Jean Vilar	Maria Casarès
Studio des Champs-Elysées	Jacques Mauclair	Jacques Mauclair, Tsilla Chelton
Petit-Marigny	J.-L. Barrault	
Quartier Latin		
Studio des Champs-Elysées	Claude Martin	R.-M. Chauffard
Atelier	André Barsacq	Jacques Duby
Mathurins	Albert Camus	Catherine Sellers
Atelier	André Barsacq	Jacques Duby
Alliance française	J.-M. Serreau	
Gramont	René Dupuy	Colette Renard
Comédie-Française	Jacques Charron	Robert Hirsch
Studio des Champs-Elysées	Roger Blin	
Alliance française	Roger Postec	décors by Siné
Comédie-Française	R. Planchon	décors by René Allio

Year	Event	Title	Author
1957 (*contd.*)		*Histoire de Vasco*	Schéhadé
		The Castle	Kafka
		Protée	Paul Claudel
		Patate	Marcel Achard
		Journal d'Anne Franck	
		La Hobereaute	Audiberti
1958		*Ubu roi*	Jarry
		A View from the Bridge	Arthur Miller
		La Bonne soupe	F. Marceau
		La Paix du dimanche	J. Osborne
		Les Caprices de Marianne	Musset
1959	J.-L. BARRAULT	*Tueur sans gages*	Ionesco
	at the Odéon	*Les Nègres*	Jean Genet
	Death of GERARD PHILIPE	*Les Séquestrés d' Altona*	J.-P. Sartre
		Tête d'Or	Paul Claudel
		Tchin-tchin	F. Billetdoux
		L'Effet Glapion	Audiberti
		L'Hurluberlu	Jean Anouilh
		Becket ou l'Honneur de Dieu	Jean Anouilh
		Les Bâtisseurs d'empire	Boris Vian
		The Possessed	Dostoïevski, Can
		Le Crapaud-Buffle	A. Gatti
		Pique-nique à la campagne	Arrabal
1960	Death of CAMUS	*Le Balcon*	Jean Genet
		Rhinocéros	Ionesco
		La Dernière bande	Beckett
		Arturo Ui	Brecht
		Antigone	Sophocles
		Le Cardinal d'Espagne	Montherlant
		La Logeuse	Audiberti
		Un Château en Suède	Françoise Sagan
		Génousie	Obaldia
		Dead Souls	Gogol, Adamov
		L'Idiote	Marcel Achard
		Boeing-Boeing	M. Camoletti
1961		*Va donc chez Törpe*	F. Billetdoux
		Naïves Hirondelles	R. Dubillard
		Le Voyage	Schéhadé
		Cher Menteur	Jerome Kilty
		Le Tricycle	Arrabal
		Les Nourrices	R. Weingarten
		Les Maxibules	Marcel Aymé
		Judith	Jean Giraudoux
		La Grotte	Jean Anouilh
		Les Bonnes	Jean Genet
		Boulevard Durand	Armand Salacrou
1962	Death of DANIEL SORANO	*La Fourmi dans le corps*	Aubiderti
		La Maison d'os	R. Dubillard
		La Vie imaginaire de l'éboueur Auguste Geai	Armand Gatti
		Le roi se meurt	Ionesco
		La Remise	Roger Planchon
		La Reine verte	M. Béjart
		La Foire d'empoigne	Jean Anouilh

Theatre	Production	Cast
Sarah-Bernhardt	J.-L. Barrault	J.-P. Granval
Sarah-Bernhardt	J.-L. Barrault	
Tertre	Serge Ligier	
Saint-Georges		Pierre Dux
Montparnasse-Gaston-Baty	M. Jamois	
Vieux-Colombier	Jean Le Poulain	Françoise Spira
TNP	Jean Vilar	G. Wilson, Rosy Varte
Antoine		
Gymnase		
Œuvre		Pierre Vaneck
TNP	Jean Vilar	Gérard Philipe, G. Page
Récamier	José Quaglio	
Lutèce	Roger Blin	Les Griots
Renaissance	F. Darbon	S. Reggiani, F. Ledoux, Evelyne Rey
Théâtre de France	J.-L. Barrault	Alain Cuny, L. Terzieff
Poche	F. Darbon	Catharina Renn
La Bruyère	G. Vitaly	
Comédie des Champs-Elysées	Roland Pietri	Paul Meurisse
Montparnasse	Jean Anouilh	D. Ivernel, Bruno Kremer
Récamier	Jean Negroni	
Antoine	Albert Camus	
Récamier	Jean Vilar	
Lutèce	J.-M. Serreau	
Gymnase	Peter Brook	Marie Bell, Loleh Bellon
Théâtre de France	J.-L. Barrault	Cle Renaud-Barrault
Récamier	Roger Blin	R.-M. Chauffard
TNP	Jean Vilar	
TNP	Jean Vilar	Catherine Sellers
Comédie-Française	Jean Mercure	Henri Rollan
Œuvre	Pierre Valde	
Atelier	André Barsacq	
Récamier	Roger Mollien	
Théâtre de France	Roger Planchon	
Saint-Georges		
Comédie-Caumartin		
Studio des Champs-Elysées	A. Bourseiller	
Poche		
Théâtre de France	J.-L. Barrault	
Athénée		P. Brasseur, M. Casarès
Poche	O. Hussenot	
Lutèce	The author	
Bouffes-Parisiens		
Théâtre de France	J.-L. Barrault	Loleh Bellon
Montparnasse	Roland Pietri	
Théâtre de France	J.-M. Serreau	
Sarah-Bernhardt	A. Reybaz	Centre dramatique du Nord
Comédie-Française		
Lutèce	the author	
Villeurbanne	Jacques Rosner	Théâtre de la Cité, Jean Bouise
Alliance française	Jacques Mauclair	
Villeurbanne	Roger Planchon	Théâtre de la Cité
Hébertot	M. Béjart	Maria Casarès
Comédie des Champs-Elysées	Jean Anouilh	

Year	Event	Title	Author
1962 (*contd.*)		*La Grande Oreille*	P.-A. Bréal
		La Guerre de Troie n'aura pas lieu	Jean Giraudoux
		Victor	Roger Vitrac
		Tartuffe	Molière
		The Hostage	Brendan Behan
			J. Paris
1963	JEAN VILAR leaves TNP	*Oh! les beaux jours*	Beckett
		Les Viaducs de la Seine-et-Oise	Marguerite Dura
		Le Piéton de l'air	Ionesco
		La Tragédie du roi Christophe	Aimé Césaire
		Printemps 71	A. Adamov
		Le Neveu de Rameau	Diderot, P. Fres
1964	Death of MARGUERITE JAMOIS	*Le Cavalier seul*	Audiberti
		Comédie	Beckett
		Il faut passer par les nuages	F. Billetdoux
		Zoo	Vercors
		Luther	J. Osborne
		Romulus the Great	Dürrenmatt
		Fando et Lis	Arrabal
		La Preuve par quatre	F. Marceau
		Croque-Monsieur	Marcel Mithois
		Fleur de cactus	Barillet-Grédy
		Le Cadavre encerclé	Kateb Yacine
		Herr Puntila and his Man Matti	Brecht
1965	Death of AUDIBERTI	*Les Eaux et forêts*	Marguerite Dur
		La Musica	Marguerite Dur
		Des journées entières dans les arbres	Marguerite Dur
		Du vent dans les branches de sassafras	Obaldia
		La Folle de Chaillot	Jean Giraudou
		L'Opéra du monde	Audiberti
		Le Goûter des généraux	Boris Vian
		Le Guerre civile	Montherlant
		Le Repos du 7e jour	Paul Claudel
		Les Paravents	Jean Genet
		La Soif et la faim	Ionesco
		L'Eté	R. Weingarten
		Le Grand Cérémonial	Arrabal
		La Promenade du dimanche	Georges Michel
		La Conversation	Claude Mauriac
		En regardant tomber les murs	Guy Foissy
		Chant public devant deux chaises électriques	Armand Gatti
		Le Cheval évanoui	Françoise Sagan
		The Idiot	Dostoïevski, Ba
		Henry VI	Shakespeare
		Marat-Sade	Peter Weiss
		La prochaine fois, je vous le chanterai	James Saunders
1967	Death of MARCEL AYMÉ	*La Tentation de saint Antoine*	Flaubert
		Silence, l'arbre remue encore	Billetdoux
		Le Labyrinthe	Arrabal
		L'Architecte et l'empereur d'Assyrie	Arrabal
		Le Silence et le mensonge	Nathalie Sarrau
		Les ancêtres redoublent de férocité	Kateb Yacine
		Dom Juan	Molière
		J'ai rencontré la vérité	F. Marceau
		The Homecoming	H. Pinter
		The Kitchen	A. Wesker

Theatre	Production	Cast
Théâtre de Paris	Jacques Fabbri	
Avignon	Jean Vilar	
Ambigu	Jean Anouilh	Claude Rich
Villeurbanne	Roger Planchon	Théâtre de la Cité
Théâtre de France	Georges Wilson	
Théâtre de France	Roger Blin	Madeleine Renaud
Poche	Claude Régy	
Théâtre de France	J.-L. Barrault	
Théâtre de France	J.-M. Serreau	
Saint-Denis	Claude Martin	
Michodière	Pierre Fresnay	Pierre Fresnay
Théâtre du Cothurne (Lyon)	Marcel Maréchal	
Pavillon de Marsan	J.-M. Serreau	
Théâtre de France	J.-L. Barrault	M. Renaud, J. Desailly
TNP	Jean Deschamps	
TNP	Georges Wilson	P. Vaneck
TNP	Georges Wilson	
Lutèce	Claude Cyriaque	
Michodière		
Saint-Georges	J.-P. Grenier	Jacqueline Maillan
Bouffes-Parisiens		
Récamier	J.-M. Serreau	
TNP	Georges Wilson	G. Wilson, Charles Denner
Mouffetard	Yves Brainville	
Studio des Champs-Elysées	Alain Astruc	
Théâtre de France	J.-L. Barrault	M. Renaud, J. Desailly
Gramont	René Dupuy	Michel Simon
TNP	Georges Wilson	Edwige Feuillère
Lutèce	Marcel Maréchal	
Gaîté-Montparnasse	François Maistre	
Œuvre	Pierre Dux	Pierre Fresnay
Œuvre	Pierre Franck	F. Ledoux, M. Casarès
Théâtre de France	Roger Blin	Maria Casarès
Comédie-Française	J.-M. Serreau	Robert Hirsch
Poche	J.-F. Adam	
Mathurins	G. Vitaly	Jean Négroni
Studio des Champs-Elysées	M. Jacquemont	
Lutèce	Nicolas Bataille	
Studio des Champs-Elysées	J.-M. Serreau	
TNP	the author	
Gymnase		
Atelier	André Barsacq	
Théâtre de France	J.-L. Barrault	décors by J. Dupont
Sarah-Bernhardt	Jean Tasso	
Antoine	Claude Régy	
Théâtre de France	Maurice Béjart	
Avignon	A. Bourseiller	Serge Reggiani
Vincennes	Jérôme Savary	
Montparnasse	Jorge Lavelli	Raymond Gérôme
Théâtre de France	J.-L. Barrault	
TNP	J.-M. Serreau	
Comédie-Française	A. Bourseiller	Jacques Charron
Comédie des Champs-Elysées		François Périer
Théâtre de Paris	Claude Régy	P. Brasseur, C. Rich
Médrano	A. Mnouchkine	Théâtre du Soleil

Year	Event	Title	Author
1968	Barrault leaves the Odéon Incidents at Avignon Festival	*A Midsummer Night's Dream* *Le Diable et le Bon Dieu* *(revival)* *L'Amante anglaise* *Akropolis* *Rabelais*	Shakespeare J.-P. Sartre M. Duras Wyspianski J.-L. Barrault
1969	SAMUEL BECKETT awarded Nobel prize	*Le Concile d'amour* *Les Clowns* *l'Avare* *Cher Antoine* *On ne sait jamais* *Le Jardin des délices* *La Mise en pièces du Cid*	Panizza group productio Molière Jean Anouilh André Roussin Arrabal Roger Planchon
1970	Death of ARTHUR ADAMOV IONESCO elected to Académie Française	*Ne Réveillez-pas madame* *Jarry sur la butte* *Marie Tudor* *1789* *Jeux de massacre* *George Dandin* *Un Piano dans l'herbe* *Alice dans les Jardins* *de Luxembourg* *Albert I* *Rintru patron tar, hin!* *La Guerre de Troie n'aura pas lieu* *Un Chapeau de paille d'Italie* *Un Petit nid d'amour*	Jean Anouilh Jarry Hugo Ariane Mnouch Ionesco Molière Sagan Weingarten Philippe Adrien Billetdoux Giraudoux Labiche Georges Miche
1971	Death of JEAN VILAR	*Les Chroniques de Zartan* *La Peau d'un fruit sur un arbre pourre* *La Cigogne* *Grand Magic Circus* *La Petite Voiture de flammes et de voix*	Jérôme Savary Victor Haïm Armand Gatti Jérôme Savary Liliane Atlan
1972	Death of PIERRE BRASSEUR	*Pucelle* *1793*	Audiberti Ariane Mnouc
1973	Death of ANDRÉ BARSACQ Death of JEAN-MARIE SERREAU	*L'Eglise* *Pardessus-Bord* *L'Ecole des femmes* *Harolde et Maude* *La Noce chez les petits-bourgeois* *Conservations dans le Loir et-Cher* *Le Voyageur sans bagages*	Céline Michel Vinave Molière Colin Higgins Brecht Paul Claudel Jean Anouilh
1974		*Dreyfus* *Ce Formidable Bordel* *Andromaque* *Les Fausses Confidences* *L'Amie rose* *Bajazet* *Le Cochon noir* *La Dispute*	J.-L. Grumber Ionesco Racine Marivaux Rene Ehni Racine Roger Plancho Marivaux

Theatre	Production	Cast
Médrano	A. Mnouchkine	Théâtre du Soleil
TNP	G. Wilson	François Périer
Gémier		C. Dauphin, M. Renaud
Epée-de-Bois	Grotowski	Théâtre de Wroclaw
Elysée-Montmartre	J.-L. Barrault	
Théâtre de Paris	J. Lavelli	
Théâtre d'Aubervilliers	A. Mnouchkine	Théâtre du Soleil
Comédie-Française	J.-P. Roussillon	Michel Aumont
Comédie des Champs-Elysées	Jean Anouilh	J. François, F. Bergé, P. Bertin, Fr. Rosay
Michodière	André Roussin	P. Fresnay, C. Minazzoli
Antoine	Claude Régy	Delphine Seyrig
Montparnasse-Gaston-Baty	Roger Planchon	Jean Bouix
Comédie des Champs-Elysées	The author	François Perrier, Daniele Lebrun
Elysée-Montmartre	J.-L. Barrault	Jacques Alric
TEP	George Werler	Rosy Varte
Vincennes		Théâtre du Soleil
Montparnasse	Jorge Lavelli	
Comédie-Française	J.-P. Roussillon	Robert Hirsch, Michel Etcheverry, Denise Gence
Atelier		
Mathurins		
Münster		
Théâtre de Paris		
Théâtre de Paris		
Théâtre de Paris		
Cie d'Aquitaine		
Galérie de la Cité, Paris		
Poche-Montparnasse		
Nanterre		
Théâtre de la Cité Internationale		
Avignon		
Hôtel de Sully, Paris		
Vincennes	Ariane Mnouchkine	Théâtre du Soleil
Théâtre de la Plaine		
TNP, Villeurbanne	Roger Planchon	Jean Bouix
Comédie-Française	J.-P. Roussillon	Pierre Dux, Michel Aumont
Récamier	J.-L. Barrault	Madeleine Renaud
Cyrano	J.-P. Vincent	
Carré Thorigny		
Mathurins		
Odéon	Jacques Rosner	Cie de Lambrequin
Moderne		
Petit-Odéon	J.-P. Roussillon	
Théâtre de la Ville		Geneviève Page
Strasbourg		
Petit Odéon		Maria Casarès
TNP Villeurbanne	Roger Planchon	
Odéon	Patrice Chéreau	

1974 *(contd.)*	*L'Excès*	Philippe Adrien (after Bataille)
	Le Cavalier seul	Audiberti
	Protée	Paul Claudel
	Toller	Tankred Dorst
	Cérémonie pour un noir assassiné	Arrabal
	Le Tartuffe	Molière
	De Moïse à Mao	Jérôme Savary
	Krapp's Last Tape ⎫	
	Comédie ⎬	Samuel Beckett
	Souffle ⎭	
	Goodbye Mr Freud	Jérôme Savary, Copi and others
	Timon of Athens	Shakespeare
	Ainsi parlait Zarathustra	J.-L. Barrault (after Nietzsche
1975	*A.A. Théâtre d'Arthur Adamov*	Planchon-Serre
	Les Caprices de Marianne	Musset
	En R'venant d'l'expo	J.-L. Grumberg

Atelier		
TEP		
Hébertot		
Odéon	Patrice Chéreau	
Théâtre de la Plaine		
Porte St Martin		Roger Planchon
Théâtre d'Orsay	Grand Magic Circus	
Théâtre de la Cité Internationale		
Porte St. Martin	Grand Magic Circus	
Bouffes du Nord	Peter Brook	
Théâtre d'Orsay	J.-L. Barrault	
TNP Villeurbanne		Cie de Strasbourg
La Renaissance	André-Louis Perinetti	
Odéon	J.-P. Vincent	

Further reading

1 GENERAL HISTORIES OF THE THEATRE
Dumur, Guy, *Histoire des spectacles* (Gallimard, 'Encyclopédie de la Pléiade', 1965).
Leclerc, Guy, *Les Grandes Aventures du théâtre* (Editeurs français réunis, 1965).
Moussinac, Léon, *Histoire du théâtre, des origines à nos jours* (Editeurs français réunis, 1961).
Pandolfi, Vito, *Histoire du théâtre* (Gérard, 'Marabout Université', Verviers, 1968–69, 4 vols).

2 HISTORIES OF CONTEMPORARY FRENCH THEATRE
Encyclopédie du théâtre contemporain (Olivier Perrin, 1959, 2 vols).
Le Théâtre moderne (C.N.R.S., 1958–67, 2 vols).
Beigbeder, Marc, *Le Théâtre en France depuis la Libération* (Bordas, 1959).
Crossvogel, David, *20th Century French Drama* (Columbia University Press, New York, 1958).
Guicharnaud, Jacques, *Modern French Theatre from Giraudoux to Genet* (University of Yale, 1967).
Lalou, Réné, *Le Théâtre en France depuis 1900* (P.U.F., 'Que sais-je?', 1951).
Simon, Alfred, *Dictionnaire du Théâtre français contemporain* (Larousse, 1970).
Simon, Pierre-Henri, *Théâtre et Destin* (Colin, 1959).
Surer, Paul, *Le Théâtre français contemporain* (C.D.U., 1964).

3 AVANT-GARDE THEATRE
Corvin, Michel, *Le Théâtre nouveau en France* (P.U.F., 'Que sais-je?', 1963).
Esslin, Martin, *The Theatre of the Absurd* (Eyre and Spottiswoode, 1962).
Henderson, John A., *The First Avant-garde 1887–1894* (Harrap, 1971).
Pronko, Leonard C., *Avant-garde Theatre* (Denoël, 1963).
Serreau, Geneviève, *Histoire du nouveau théâtre* (Gallimard, 'Idées', 1966).

4 GENERAL STUDIES
Notre théâtre: théâtre moderne, public populaire (*Esprit*, numéro special de mai, 1965).
Aslan, Odette, *L'Art du théâtre* (Seghers, 1963).
Baecque, André de, *Le Théâtre d'aujourd'hui* (Seghers, 1964).
Dort, Bernard, *Théâtre public* (Seuil, 1967).

Fletcher, John, *Twentieth Century French Drama* (University of London Press, 1972).

Hobson, Harold, *The French Theatre of Today* (Harrap, 1953).

Madral, Philippe, *Le Théâtre hors les murs* (Seuil, 1969).

Roy, Claude, *L'Amour du théâtre* (Gallimard, 1965).

Temkine, Raymonde, *L'Entreprise théâtre* (Cujas, 1967).

5 Philosophy of Theatre

Clark, Barrett H., *European Theories of the Drama* (Crown, 1965).

Domenach, Jean-Marie, *Le Retour du tragique* (Seuil, 1967).

Duvignaud, Jean, *Sociologie du théâtre* (P.U.F., 1965).

Duvignaud, Jean, *L'Acteur, Esquisse d'une sociologie du comédien* (Gallimard, 1965).

Gouhier, Henri, *Présence du théâtre* (Plon, 1943).

Gouhier, Henri, *Le Théâtre et l'existence* (Aubier, 1952).

Steiner, George, *The Death of Tragedy* (Faber, 1961).

Touchard, Pierre-Aimé, *Dionysos, apologie pour le théâtre* (Seuil, 1949, 2nd edn., 1968).

6 Technique

Moussinac, Leon, *Traité de mise en scène* (Libr. centrale des Beaux-arts, 1948).

Sonrel, Pierre, *Traité de scénographie* (Odette Lieutier, 1944).

Veinstein, André, *La Mise en scène théâtrale et sa condition esthétique* (Flammarion, 1955).

7 On Directors

Anders, France, *Jacques Copeau et le cartel des quatre* (Nizet, 1959).

Arnaud, Lucien, *Charles Dullin* (L'Arche, 'le Théâtre et les jours', 1953).

Frank, André, *Georges Pitoëff* (L'Arche, 'le Théâtre et les jours', 1958).

Robichez, Jacques, *Lugné-Poe* (L'Arche, le Théâtre et les jours', 1955).

Roussou, Matei, *André Antoine* (L'Arche, 'le Théâtre et les jours', 1954).

Roy, Claude, *Jean Vilar* (Seghers, 1968).

8 On Dramatists

Albérès, René-Marill, *Esthétique et morale de Jean Giraudoux* (Nizet, 1957).

Alter, André, *Paul Claudel* (Seghers, 1967).

Benmussa, Simone, *Ionesco* (Seghers, 1966).

Brustein, Robert, 'Antonin Artaud and Jean Genet: the Theatre of Cruelty', in *The Theatre of Revolt* (Boston, 1964).

Coe, Richard N., *Ionesco* (Methuen, 1961).

Farabet, René, *Le Jeu de l'acteur dans le théâtre de Claudel* (Les Lettres modernes, 1960).

Inskip, Donald, *Jean Giraudoux, the Making of a Dramatist* (London, 1958).

Madaule, Jacques, *Le Drame de Paul Claudel* (Desclée de Brouwer et Cie, 1935).

Madaule, Jacques, *Paul Claudel Dramaturge* (L'Arche, 1956).

9 BOOKS BY IMPORTANT FIGURES

Artaud, Antonin, *Le Théâtre et son double* (Gallimard, 'Idées', 1966).
Barrault, Jean-Louis, *Souvenirs pour demain* (Gallimard, 1972).
Dullin, Charles, *Souvenirs et notes de travail d'un acteur* (Odette Lieutier, 1946).
Ionesco, Eugène, *Notes et contre-notes* (Gallimard, 'Idées', 1966).
Jouvet, Louis, *Le Comédien désincarné* (Flammarion, 1953).
Jouvet, Louis, *Témoignages sur le théâtre*, (Flammarion, 1952).
Sartre, Jean-Paul, *Un Théâtre de situations* (Gallimard, 'Idées', 1973).
Vilar, Jean, *De la tradition théâtrale* (L'Arche, 1955).

Selected list of plays

Adamov, Arthur
Théâtre, 3 vols., Paris: Gallimard, 1953–66

Adrien, Philippe
La Baye, Paris: Editions du Seuil, 1968
Albert Ier, Paris: Editions du Seuil, 1969

Anouilh, Jean
Pièces noires, Paris: La Table Ronde, 1967
Pièces roses, Paris, Calmann-Lévy, 1945
Nouvelles Pièces noires, Paris: La Table Ronde, 1967
Pièces brillantes, Paris: La Table Ronde, 1965
Pièces grinçantes, Paris: La Table Ronde, 1966
L'Hurluberlu, Paris: La Table Ronde, 1959
Pièces Costumées, Paris: La Table Ronde, 1967
Ne réveillez-pas Madame . . . Paris: La Table Ronde, 1966

Artaud, Antonin
Oeuvres Complètes, vols I–XI, Paris: Gallimard, 1956–74

Arrabal, Fernando
Théâtre, 5 vols., Paris: Christian Bourgois, 1967–69

Atlan, Liliane
Monsieur Fugue ou le mal de terre, Paris: Editions du Seuil, 1969

Audiberti, Jacques
Théâtre, 5 vols., Paris: Gallimard 1948–62

Beckett, Samuel
En attendant Godot, Paris: Editions de Minuit, 1952
Fin de Partie suivi de Acte Sans Paroles, Paris: Editions de Minuit, 1957
Oh les Beaux, Jours, Paris: Editions de Minuit, 1963
All that Fall, London: Faber & Faber, 1957
Krapp's Last Tape and Embers, London: Faber & Faber, 1959
Comédie et Actes Divers, Paris: Edition de Minuit, 1966
Eh Joe and Other Writings, London: Faber & Faber, 1967
Breath and Other Shorts, London: Faber & Faber, 1971

Benedetto, André
Zone rouge, Paris: Editions P. J. Oswald, 1969
Le Petit Train de Monsieur Kamode, Paris: Editions P. J. Oswald, 1969
Emballage, Paris: Editions P. J. Oswald, 1971

Césaire, Aimé
Une Saison au Congo, Paris: Editions du Seuil, 1967

114

Claudel, Paul
Théâtre, 2 vols., Paris: Gallimard, Pléiade, 1956

Cocteau, Jean
Théâtre complet, 2 vols., Paris: Grasset, 1957

Cousin, Gabriel
L'Opéra noir, Paris: Gallimard, 1968
Le Cycle du Crabe, Paris: Gallimard, 1969

Duras, Marguerite
Des Journées Entières dans les Arbres, Paris: Gallimard, 1954
Théâtre I, Paris: Gallimard, 1965
L'Amante Anglaise, Paris: Gallimard, 1967
India Song, Paris: Gallimard, 1974

Ehni, René
Que Ferez-Vous en Novembre, Paris: Christian Bourgois, 1968

Gatti, Armand
La Vie imaginaire de l'éboueur Auguste G., Paris: Editions du Seuil
Chant Public devant deux chaises électriques, Paris: Editions du Seuil, 1964

Genet, Jean
Haute Surveillance, Paris: Gallimard, 1949
Les Bonnes, Décines: L'Arbalète, 1958
Le Balcon, Décines: L'Arbalète, 1960
Les Nègres, Clownerie, Décines: L'Arbalète, 1958
Les Paravents, Décines: L'Arbalète, 1961

Giraudoux, Jean
Théâtre complet, 16 vols., Neuchâtel and Paris; Ides et Calendes, 1945–51

Grumberg, Jean-Claude
Amorphe d'Ottenbourg, Paris: Editions Stock
Dreyfus, Paris: Editions Stock

Ionesco, Eugène
Théâtre, 5 vols., Paris: Gallimard 1954–66

Michel, Georges
L'Agression, Paris: Gallimard, 1968
Arbalète et Vieilles Rapières, Paris: Gallimard, 1969

Montherlant, Henri de
L'Exil, Paris: Gallimard, 1929
Fils des Autres, Paris: Gallimard, 1939
La Reine morte, Paris: Gallimard, 1942
Fils de Personne, Paris: Gallimard, 1944
Malatesta, Paris: Gallimard, 1946
Le Maître de Santiago, Paris: Gallimard, 1947
Demain il fera jour, Paris: Gallimard, 1949
La Ville dont le Prince est un enfant, Paris: Gallimard, 1951
Port Royal, Paris: Gallimard, 1954
Le Cardinal d'Espagne, Paris: Gallimard, 1960
La Guerre civile, Paris: Gallimard, 1965

Planchon, Roger
Bleus, Blancs, Rouges, Paris: Gallimard, 1969
Le Cochon noir, Paris: Gallimard, 1974

Sartre, Jean-Paul
Théâtre I, Paris: Gallimard, 1947
Les Mains sales, Paris: Gallimard, 1948
Le Diable et le Bon Dieu, Paris: Gallimard, 1952
Kean, Paris: Gallimard, 1954
Nekrassov, Paris: Gallimard, 1957
Les Séquestrés d'Altona, Paris: Gallimard, 1959

Tardieu, Jean
Théâtre de Chambre, I, Paris: Gallimard, 1955
Théâtre II: Poèmes à Jouer, Paris: Gallimard, 1960

Vian, Boris
Théâtre, Paris: Pauvert, 1965
Théâtre inédit, Paris: Christian Bourgois, 1970

Yacine, Kateb
Les Ancêtres redoublent de férocité, Paris: Collection TNP

Index

Absidiole, l', 74
Achard, Marcel, 1, 63
Adamov, Arthur, 1, 8, 9, 24, 32, 40f, 86
Adrien, Phillippe, 19, 63f, 128
Aeschylus, 14
Albee, Edward, 8
Algérie Française, 22
Amiens Manifesto, 1
Anouilh, Jean, 1, 7, 14, 16, 52, 75f, 85
Antoine, André, 9
Apollinaire, Guillaume, 20
Arden, John, 8, 66
Aristophanes, 74
Aristotle, 73
Arrabal, Fernando, 1, 9, 49f, 71
Artaud, Antonin, 7, 9, 10, 11, 13, 19f, 41, 46, 83, 85, 86
Atlan, Liliane, 65f
Audiberti, Jacques, 1, 11f, 16, 41
Avignon Festival, 18
Aymé, Marcel, 1

Badel, Alan, 92
Baratier, Jacques, 45, 86
Barillet, Pierre, 1, 63
Barrault, Jean-Louis, 8, 13f, 16, 17, 32, 42, 69, 82, 84f, 92f
Bataille, Nicolas, 46
Baty, Gaston, 43, 82, 83
Beckett, Samuel, 1, 7, 8, 9f, 16, 17, 40, 51f, 60, 62, 64, 77, 85, 86, 92, 93
Bell, Marie, 94
Benedetto, André, 71f
Biasini, E. J., 3
Billetdoux, François, 1, 63, 85
Blake, William, 56
Blin, Roger, 51, 86, 87
Bogar, 17f
Bonaparte, Napoleon, 88
Bonnard, 36
Bouisse, Jean, 94
Bourseiller, Antoine, 84
Brasseur, Pierre, 94
Brecht, Bertold, 7, 9, 10, 13, 14, 17, 18f, 25, 34, 41, 43, 64, 73, 84, 87, 88f, 94
Brook, Peter, 9, 20, 51, 52, 72, 87, 91, 94
Büchner, Georg, 87
Bunuel, Luis, 49
Byron, Lord, 36

Café Théâtre, 74
Camoletti, Marc, 63
Camus, Albert, 1, 8, 9, 14, 41, 76, 78, 86

Cartel, le, 82
Cassel, Jean-Pierre, 94
Céline, Ferdinand, 23, 24
Cellini, 36
Césaire, Aimé, 8, 32f, 34, 71, 87
César, 49
Chagall, Marc, 83
Chandler, Raymond, 46
Chateaubriand, 94
Chekhov, Anton, 67
Chéreau, Patrice, 89f
Choice, Theatre of, 22f, 35f
Chopin, Frédèric, 77
Claudel, Paul, 7, 10, 11, 13f, 23, 41, 77, 84f
Cocteau, Jean, 1, 16, 17, 46, 60, 82, 85, 86, 91
Comédie Française, 4, 5, 6, 7, 38, 39, 84, 89, 94
Commedia dell'arte, 77, 83
Conservatoire, la, 7
Copeau, Jacques, 8, 20, 53, 83, 84, 87, 94f
Cosmos, Jean, 7, 65
Cousin, Gabriel, 1, 71
Corbusier, le, 3
Corneille, Pierre, 6, 39
Coward, Noël, 8
Cromer, Lord, 22
C.R.S., 22
Cruelty, Theatre of, 20f, 74, 91, 94

Dali, Salvador, 49
Dandin, Georges, 94
D'Annunzio, Gabriel, 37
Da Vinci, Leonardo, 57
De Beauvoir, Simone, 1, 9, 28, 35
Decroux, Etienne, 53, 92, 94
De Gaulle, Charles, 14, 22, 32
De Mandiargues, Pierre, 49
De Sade, Marquis, 90
De Saint Fleur, Antoine, 78
Déscrières, Georges, 94
Deval, Jacques, 1
Devine, George, 9
Diderot, Denis, 24
Donne, John, 53
Druon, Maurice, 24
Dubillard, Roland, 1
Dubois, Marie, 94
Duhamél, Jacques, 24
Dullin, Charles, 25, 82, 86
Duras, Marguerite, 1, 8, 19, 59f, 71
Dutourd, Jean, 79, 80

Ehni, René, 1, 19, 69f

Eliot, T. S., 54, 86, 87
Ernst, Max, 19
Esslin, Martin, 24, 41, 42, 47, 52, 86
Euripides, 25, 27

Faye, Jean-Pierre, 1
Feuillère, Edwige, 17, 94
Flaubert, Gustav, 82
Fletcher, John, 51
Flon, Suzanne, 94
Flores, Manuel M, 54
Foissy, Guy, 1
Forest, 49
Franco, General, 23
French Theatre Centre, 1
Friedman, Melvin, 51
Frisch, Max, 87
Fry, Christopher, 8, 12, 77

Garaudy, R., 1
Garcia, Victor, 50
Gatti, Armand, 1, 8, 19, 21, 23, 65, 71, 87, 94
Gautier, Jean-Jacques, 7, 78
Gelber, Jack, 8, 83
Genet, Jean, 1, 7, 9, 17, 21, 31, 34, 51, 52, 56f, 85, 86, 92, 94
Géricault, 90
Gignoux, H., 76
Giradoux, Jean, 16f, 23, 25, 87
Godard, Jean-Luc, 74
Gogol, Nikolai, 7
Grand Magic Circus, 8
Grédy, 1, 63
Green, Julien, 1
Greene, Graham, 30
Griffiths, Trevor, 23, 69
Group Theatre, 63
Grumberg, J-C., 1, 19, 62, 67f
Guild, The, 7
Guitry, Sacha, 77

Haïm, Victor, 1, 19, 65f, 67
Halet, Pierre, 1
Hall, Peter, 9, 51
Handke, Peter, 21
Hare, David, 9
Heidegger, Martin, 41f
Henze, Hans Werner, 24
Hirsch, Robert, 6, 89, 94
Hirt, Eléonore, 94
Hobson, Harold, 36, 79
Hugo, Victor, 7, 44

Ibsen, Henrik, 66
Ionesco, Eugène, 1, 8, 40, 42–45, 47, 64, 74, 83, 85, 87

Jarry, Alfred, 20, 47, 86
Jones, Leroi, 8
Jouvet, Louis, 17, 30, 75, 82, 83
Joyce, James, 51f, 55f

Kafka, Franz, 85, 86
Kantners, Robert, 13
Keats, John, 36
Kustow, Michael, 87

Lambreaux, Alain, 26
Lavelli, George, 16, 49
Leclerc, Guy, 31f
Lecoq, Jaques, 94
Littlewood, Joan, 65
Living Theatre, 10, 21
Louis XIV, 4, 81
Louis XVI, 88

Maisons de la Culture, 3f, 71
Mallarmé, Stephane, 20
Malraux, André, 32, 69, 85
Marceau, Felicien, 1, 2, 63
Marivaux, Pierre, 6, 90
Marowitz, Charles, 20
Marx, Karl, 72
Maulnier Thierry, 1
Mauriac, François, 1
Maurois, André, 1
Mayakowsky, 89
McWhinnie, Donald, 51
Méliès, 82
Mercer, David, 37
Michelangelo, 52
Michaux, Henri, 1, 83
Michel, Georges, 1, 31, 34, 71
Miguer, Jean-Pierre, 62
Miller, Arthur, 8
Ministry of Culture, 4, 6, 7, 24
Mithois, Marcel, 63
Mnouchkine, Ariane, 3, 8, 19, 25, 65, 72, 91
Moatti, Jacqueline, 27
Molière, Jean-Baptiste, 4, 6, 16, 78, 79, 80, 82, 84
Montherlant, Henri de, 1, 6, 7f, 24, 35f, 52, 76
Mrożek, Slawomir, 74

Nadar, 82
National Theatre, London, 69
Nietzsche, Friedrich, 14

O.A.S., 22
Obaldia, René di, 1, 74
Odets, Clifford, 68
Olivier, Oliver O., 49
Open Space Theatre, 50
Osborne, John, 8, 80

Pagnol, Marcel, 1
Panic, Theatre of, 49
Pariscope, 74
Passeur, Steve, 1
Paulhan, Jean, 20
Périer, François, 94
Permissiveness, 8, 46f
Philipe, Gérard, 94
Piaf, Edith, 46
Pichette, Henri, 1
Pinget, Robert, 74
Pinter, Harold, 8, 9, 40
Pirandello, Luigi, 89
Pitöeff, Georges, 82
Planchon, Roger, 7, 18, 19, 65, 73, 84, 87f, 94
Plato, 69
Poirot-Delpech, B., 7, 65, 85, 86

Porter, Andrew, 24
Pompidou, President, 23, 84
Proust, Marcel, 52, 54, 55, 60

Rabanne, Paco, 49
Rabelais, François, 65, 92
Racine, Jean, 39
Radine, Serge, 77
Rattigan, Terence, 8
Renaud, Madeleine, 13, 59, 85, 93
Rhétoré, Guy, 7, 18
Richardson, Jack, 8
Robespierre, Maximilien de, 88
Roger-Ferdinand, 1
Romains, Jules, 1
Rouault, Georges, 11
Roussin, André, 1, 2, 63
Rozental, Geneviève, 2, 62
Royal Court, London, 9
Royal Shakespeare Company, 46, 65
Rudkin, David, 57
Rufus, 94

Sabattini, Rafael, 82
Sachs, Dr. Oliver, 53
Sagan, Françoise, 1, 63
Saint-Denis, Michel, 9, 84
Salacrou, Armand, 1
Sarment, 1
Sartre, Jean-Paul, 1, 2, 7, 9, 11, 16, 18, 19, 22,
    23, 24f, 34, 40, 41, 55, 56, 57, 72, 76, 78, 81,
    83, 86, 87, 92
Sauvajon, M. G., 1
Savary, Jérome, 8, 49, 91
Schéhadé, Georges, 1
Sélénite, La, 74
Serreau, Jean-Marie, 86
Seyrig, Delphine, 94
Shakespeare, William, 16, 28, 76
Shaw, George Bernard, 26, 77
Shepard, Sam, 8
Simon, Alfred, 14
Society of Playwrights, 62, 63
Solzhenitsyn, Alexander, 10
Sophocles, 79
Spillane, Mickey, 46
Spurling, John, 51

Stanislavski, Constantin, 94
Steiner, George, 13, 24
Stendhal, 92
Stoppard, Tom, 8, 40
Storey, David, 8, 9
Strehler, G., 74
Sullivan, Vernon, *see* Vian, Boris

Tardieu, Jean, 1, 44, 47f, 74
Théâtre de l'Est Parisien (TEP), 4, 7, 13
Théâtre de France (l'Odéon), 4f, 13, 67, 69
Théâtre Michel, 39
Théâtre Nationale Populaire (TNP), 5, 17, 18,
    20, 30, 34, 71, 73, 87, 89, 94
Théâtre du Soleil, 3, 8, 10, 25, 30, 72
Thierry, Augustin, 79
Thomas, Dylan, 46
Thomas, M., 1
Troupe Royale, 4
Tynan, Kenneth, 2, 7

Vailland, Roger, 1
Valde, Pierre, 65
Von Hofmannsthal, Hugo, 74
Vauthier, Jean, 1
Vian, Boris, 8, 45, 46f
Vilar, Jean, 3, 7, 17, 18, 19, 20, 36, 84, 87, 89, 94
Vinaver, Michel, 1, 65, 73
Voltaire, 88

Wardle, Irving, 79
Webb, Eugène; 51
Weingarten, Romain, 1, 8, 9, 45f, 64, 71
Weiss, Peter, 88
Welles, Orson, 85
Wesker, Arnold, 8, 9, 37, 68, 72, 91
Whiting, John, 35
Williams, Tennessee, 8, 74
Williamson, Nicol, 92
Wittgenstein, Ludwig, 53
Wogensky, 3
Worms, Janine, 1

Yacine, Kateb, 1, 32, 34, 87
Yeats, W. B., 20

Zimmer, B., 1
Zola, Emile, 82